The Chris G to Your Mom

Marilyn C. Hilton

Dedication
For my mom, Lois, and all the people she loves.

Acknowledgments
With many thanks and hugs to my family for their love, all the girls and moms who shared their stories, California Girl Scout Troop 92, and awesome editor Christy Scannell.

THE CHRISTIAN GIRL'S GUIDE TO YOUR MOM
©2014 by Marilyn C. Hilton, thirteenth printing
ISBN 10: 1-58411-045-7
ISBN 13: 978-1-58411-045-3
RoseKidz® reorder# L48214
JUVENILE NONFICTION / Religion / Christianity / Christian Life

RoseKidz®
An imprint of Rose Publishing, Inc.
17909 Adria Maru Lane
Carson, CA 90746
www.Rose-Publishing.com

Cover and Interior Illustrator: Anita DuFalla

Scriptures are from the *Holy Bible: New International Version* (North American Edition), ©1973, 1978, 1984 by the International Bible Society. Used by permission of Zondervan Bible Publishers.

Printed in China

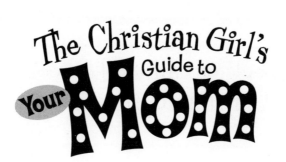

The Christian Girl's Guide to Your Mom

An imprint of Rose Publishing, Inc.
Carson, CA
www.Rose-Publishing.com

Check out all of the books in The Christian Girl's Guide series:

The Christian Girl's Guide to Being Your Best

The Christian Girl's Guide to Friendship

The Christian Girl's Guide to the Bible

The Christian Girl's Guide to Your Mom

The Christian Girl's Guide to Money

The Christian Girl's Guide to Change

The Christian Girl's Guide to Style

The Christian Girl's Guide to Me: The Quiz Book

The Girl's Guide to Your Dream Room

The Girl's Guide to Manners

Table of Contents

Dear Daughter 7

Fact 1:   She's Mom 9

Fact 2:   Mom Cares About Me 29

Fact 3:   I Can Talk with Mom 41

Fact 4:   Mom Is Proud of Me 55

Fact 5:   Mom Doesn't Expect Me to
            Be Perfect 69

Fact 6:   Mom Can Trust Me (and I
            can trust her) 84

Fact 7:   Mom Doesn't Know Everything
            (but she knows a lot!) 99

Fact 8:   I Can Play by Mom's Rules
            (and still have fun!) 112

Fact 9:   Mom Forgives Me and
            I Forgive Mom.......................124

Fact 10:   Mom Needs My Help 140

Fact 11:   Mom Is Always on
            My Side 155

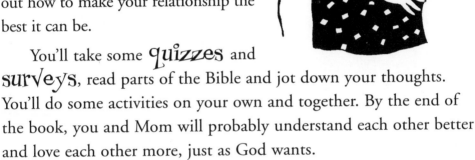

Dear Daughter,

Welcome! This book is about you & Mom. That's your mom, not your best friend's mom or the mom who drives the carpool or the one who leads your Bible study. This book will help both of you figure out how to make your relationship the best it can be.

You'll take some quizzes and surveys, read parts of the Bible and jot down your thoughts. You'll do some activities on your own and together. By the end of the book, you and Mom will probably understand each other better and love each other more, just as God wants.

You can use this book at any pace you want. For example, you can start by reading one chapter each week. Then adjust your pace to one that feels most comfortable for you.

You can do this book entirely by yourself, or with Mom.

There's plenty of space to write in this book. But if you'd rather have your very own space to write, you can use a diary, journal or notebook.

Are you ready? Let's start!

Dear friends, since God so loved us, we also ought to love one another.
                                                ~1 John 4:11

Her children arise and call her blessed.

~ Proverbs 31:28

She's Mom.

She's Mom.

i know because...

* She answers to "Mom" (or something like that).

* She prays when the dishwasher leaks, the cat's on the roof, her boss is on the phone, the baby just spit up again and I can't find my homework.

* She uses drive-through windows for burgers, prescriptions, dry-cleaning and doughnuts.

* When she's mad she calls me by my full name.

There's no doubt about it—the woman in your house who sometimes calls you by your full name, who drives you all around town, who teaches you how to keep the red socks out of the white laundry load and who somehow does a week's worth of chores and activities in one day before crashing into bed—is Mom.

By now, you've spent several years together. But, how well do you know her? She's your mom (and she wouldn't trade that for anything), but she's many other things, too. For example, she could be any or all of these: a Christian, a wife, a friend, a daughter, a sister, a church member (possibly a church leader) and an employee. She might be a stepmom, a widow or a grandma.

God has given you and your mom a very special relationship. Sometimes your relationship with your mom feels like the warmest and closest one you'd ever want, and other times it might not seem so special at all. You might think Mom understands you completely, gives you everything you ask for and does everything you want. At other times, she gets in the way of all your fun and seems to have no idea what it's like to be your age.

I like Mom because she takes care of our family. She shares her faith with me by going to church.

— JuLia K.
age 12
CaliFornia

But Mom does know what it's like to be your age, because not too long ago she WAS a girl your age. If you ask her what her life was like then, she can probably talk about it as if it were last year. Sure, she wore different kinds of clothes and hairstyles, listened to different music and used different words than you do to describe things in her life, but she had the same hopes and dreams that you do, felt the same joys, frustrations and disappointments and prayed the same kinds of prayers. Mom asks God for the same things for you that your grandma asked for Mom.

Let's spend some time looking at you and Mom from both sides, and then see how God is an essential part of this incredibly important relationship.

The Two of You

Mom

She makes you giggle, but sometimes she drives you nuts. She's sweet yet crabby at times. You love her, but you think she doesn't always understand what you say or how you feel. One minute you're both getting along great, and the next minute you can't believe she just said THAT. (And sometimes you can't believe YOU just said that!)

She works at home, and maybe she also works in an office, a restaurant, a factory or a hospital. She's married to your dad, or your stepdad or she's not married to anyone.

She's tall, short, slender, plump, soft, toned. She races around like her hair's on fire, or she's as slow as a turtle getting everything done.

She's silly, serious and maybe even a little embarrassing.

Sometimes she says things that are either really old-fashioned or just way too cool.

She dresses in her own style, or one straight out of the magazines or maybe in your style.

Mom says things like:

✳ "This isn't an all-night diner."

✳ "Take a number."

✳ "You're my grown-up girl."

✳ "This room looks like a toxic waste dump."

✳ "Don't swallow your gum because it stays in your stomach forever."

✳ "Will her parents be home?"

✳ "You are beautiful through and through."

✳ "Hurry uuuup! We're gonna be laaaate!"

✳ "I love you with all my heart."

✳ "Hold your horses, please. I don't have four hands/three heads/five legs."

✳ "You've already got a zillion pairs of shoes!"

✳ "That's not a good web site for you."

✳ "I don't know where your P.E. shorts are. Do I look like Sherlock Holmes?"

✳ "You'll always be my baby."

Bar*mom*eter 1

See how well you know Mom by predicting how she might react to different situations. Think about each example below, and then circle the answer that best describes her.

1. You have to finish a book report before dinner because you want to go to youth group tonight. But you forget to set the table (one of your chores) – for the third time this week! Mom:

a. sets the table for you, as usual, and says she understands.

b. sets the table for you but says you can't go out tonight.

c. sets everyone's place except yours, says you can't go out tonight and takes money out of your allowance.

d. grounds you for a week.

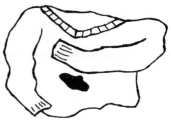

2. You plan to wear your teal blue sweater to a party on Saturday night. At 4:00 that day you remember you left it in the bottom of your closet with a big salsa stain on it. Mom:

a. rushes the sweater to the one-hour cleaners.

b. tells you to choose a different sweater and be prepared to pay the cleaning bill.

c. picks out the ugliest sweater to wear, and lectures you about responsibility.

d. says you can't go to the party.

3. Mom doesn't want you to hang out with a particular girl because she uses rough language and wears "inappropriate" clothes. You like the girl anyway and think you can be a good example for her. Mom:

a. gives in quickly–you can see her anytime, anywhere.

b. suggests you invite her to church, but that's the only way you can spend time with her.

c. tells you she can come to your house but only when she or Dad is home.

d. says the case is closed and won't talk about it anymore.

4. You're invited to a sleepover, but you heard that boys have also been invited. You don't want to look dumb and say "no," but the idea of a mixed sleepover makes you really uncomfortable. Mom:

a. says it's okay, as long as the parents are there all night.

b. asks you how you feel about it.

c. says you can go if you want to, but only until 11:00.

d. immediately calls the parents and tells them they're out of their minds.

5. Aunt Leslie pops in with your creepy cousin Ian just as you're heading out to your friend Taylor's house. Mom:

a. waves you out the back door without a word.

b. tells you to say your hello's and then you can go.

c. suggests you invite Taylor to your house so you can both hang out with Ian.

d. tells you to cancel your plans for the evening.

Count the number of a, b, c and d answers.

❋ If you answered all or mostly "a," Mom trusts you to make your own choices in most situations. If this is okay with you, then the two of you should get along fine. You can predict that she'll rely on you to make the right choices. If you want more help knowing what's right or wrong, tell her so.

❋ If you answered all or mostly "b," Mom trusts you most of the time to make the right choices and helps you see other possibilities. You can predict that she'll make decisions for the little things and leave the big decisions to you. If you want more input from her, tell her so.

❋ If you answered all or mostly "c," Mom wants to continue teaching and guiding you as you grow into your teens. She offers you fewer alternatives and makes her preferences clear. You can predict that she'll make most decisions for you and leave the little ones to you. If you want more control over what happens, tell her so.

✳ If you answered all or mostly "d," Mom shows her love for you by making almost every decision for you. You may see this style as too rigid, with few choices for you to make. But Mom sees it as protecting you from harm. You can predict that she'll decide just about everything for you. If you want more control, tell her why your choices make sense for you and show that you can make the right choices.

✳ If your answers were mixed, Mom uses a combination of all these styles. She responds to each situation individually. She's harder to predict, but her style might also be easier to adapt to.

You

You're not a little girl anymore, and the things you liked to do a few years ago are boring or too childish now. You probably like to talk on the phone, email and IM with your friends. You also like to spend time by yourself in your room thinking, reading or listening to music.

Sometimes Mom treats you like a kid, and sometimes she expects you to think and act like you're older. It's confusing because even though you just want to be left alone, you still want Mom to be there for you and take care of you.

Do any of these sound like you?

✳ "I used to think Mom was perfect. Now I'm not so sure. What happened?"

✳ "Mom really embarrasses me with what she says or does sometimes."

✳ "When I want to talk, it's hard to get her attention because she's always busy or tired."

✳ "I want to grow up but she doesn't seem to want me to."

✳ "She always asks me about my friends, won't let me go on dates and criticizes my clothes and my music."

✳ "I can't talk to her about things like bras and periods. I'd rather talk to my best friend about those things."

✳ "Sometimes Mom and Dad fight, and it makes me feel sad and scared. How can I get them to stop?"

✳ "I can't imagine Mom ever being my age. She's so old!"

Understanding Mom during this time can be confusing. Growing up isn't easy!

FAQs

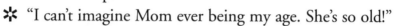

Q: My mom and dad adopted me when I was a baby. Now Mom's having a baby of her own. I'm scared that they won't love me as much.

A: You say your mom is having a baby of her own, but that's exactly what you are to her. When your mom and dad adopted you, they chose you to be their very own. They would not have loved you any more if your mom had given birth to you. When the new baby comes, expect some changes in your family. These changes won't come because your mom and dad stop loving you, but because having a new baby changes a family's routine. Your parents might have less time to spend with you or be more tired, but as your little brother or sister grows, life will get easier for all of you. In the meantime, you can show love to your mom by asking her to teach you how to change a diaper, feed with a bottle and bathe the baby. All these things will give your mom more time and energy for you. And, the more time you spend with your new brother or sister, the better you will know each other. Your mom will be even more proud of you for being a good sibling!

Q: I love my mom. I love my dad, too. Sometimes I get the feeling that Mom is jealous of Dad when he and I spend more time together and talk about things that she and I don't. What can I do?

A: Think of it this way: your mom carried you in her body for nine months, and then took care of you night and day for many years.

I was adopted when I was a baby. My mom says God brought us together. It's funny when we're out and someone says we look alike because we don't at all except we both have blonde hair.

—Bethany L.
age 10
Illinois

You've always depended on her and you still need her to help you get through the rest of your growing-up years. But you're also seeking the special love and feedback of your dad, and your mom feels left out of conversations and situations in which she used to play a major role. She wonders if you need her anymore–or even if you love her as much as you loved her as a little kid. She might even be more aware of her own faults and shortcomings now that you're old enough to see them and form opinions of her. What can you do? Go on errands now and then with her if you have a choice, suggest things you can do together and tell her you love her. Explain to her how you feel and what you're thinking. She wants you to have a strong, positive relationship with your dad, but she also wants to know that you still need her.

Q: Mom still wants to stand with me in the school line and walk me to my classroom. That was fine when I was little, but now I'm in fifth grade. It's so embarrassing. How can I get her to stop?

A: Moms are torn between doing everything for you to protect you and allowing you to be more independent. Your mom knows she has to let you go but doesn't know exactly when to start— especially if you're the oldest child in the family because she hasn't gone through this "letting go" stuff yet! That said, at fifth grade you are probably old enough to stand in

line by yourself and walk in to school with your classmates. Ask your mom for a compromise. At the least, she could see you to the school gates or the playground edge and say good-bye there. If it embarrasses you when she kisses and hugs you in front of your friends, kiss her when you leave the house or the car (before you open the door), or agree on a code phrase that means "I love you" (such as "Did you feed the goldfish?"). That way you will always begin your day with a laugh!

"Before" Snapshot

A "snapshot" shows things the way they were at a particular moment. By answering the questions on the next page, you can take a snapshot of Mom. (At the end of the book you'll take another one to compare.)

1. Set a timer for one minute, and on a sheet of paper write adjectives that describe Mom. Focus on her personality more than her looks. Write as many as you can before time's up (use another sheet of paper if you need it).

_____   _____

_____   _____

_____   _____

Now look at the adjectives you wrote. Do you see mostly positive words, negative words or a good mix? Put a checkmark next to each positive adjective. Look closely at each negative one. How would God lovingly reword each one? (For example, "lazy" could be "exhausted" or "bossy" might be "protective.") Write your reword next to your first word.

Mum's The Word!

In Albanian: Mami
In Bulgarian: Mama
In Serbian: Majka
In Xhosa: Umama

2. Do the same for yourself. In one minute, write on a sheet of paper as many adjectives as you can about you. Checkmark the positive ones, then reword the negatives.

_____   _____

_____   _____

_____   _____

_____   _____

3. Earlier, you read some things a mom might say. Now write some that Mom says – good, bad, funny, sad, confusing and so on.

_____

_____

_____

_____

4. In the space on the next page, draw a picture of Mom that shows her the way you see her. If you don't want to draw, glue a picture from a magazine or use a photograph.

 Picture of Mom

He's God

Being a mom is the best job in the world, but it can be difficult—especially when her daughter is growing and changing as fast as a sunflower. Yesterday you were her baby and depended on her for everything. When she looks at you today and she sees the lovely young woman you're becoming, she's torn between holding onto you and giving you more space.

You've probably heard the expression "Children don't come with instructions." It means that parents don't get much formal training on how to raise their children—they have to learn as they go along. Just the same, moms don't come with instructions either, so you have to learn how to be a good daughter as you go along, too.

Actually, there is an instruction book for you both: the Bible! It's full of information on being a good daughter and mom written by God, the greatest teacher you'll ever know.

God is concerned about everything in your life, including your relationship with Mom. He wants you to talk with each other, laugh with each other and love each other forever. God is always in control of every situation. He has a reason for everything He does, including why He put you and Mom together. You may never know why, but you can relax and feel confident knowing that God is great, good and always knows what He's doing.

Ruth and Naomi

Ruth's name means:
friend (in Hebrew)
Naomi's name means:
pleasant (also in Hebrew)
Ruth was born in: Moab, a land southeast of the Dead Sea and Bethlehem
Naomi was born in: we don't know, but she lived in Bethlehem (in Judah, a kingdom in southern Palestine)
Sister-in-law: Orpah (not Oprah!)
Ruth's husband: Mahlon, Naomi's son
Naomi's husband: Elimelech

Ruth lived in Moab with her mom and dad. She and Orpah, another girl from Moab, married two brothers, Mahlon and Chilion, who had fled to Moab with their parents, Naomi and Elimelech, during a great famine in Judah. Neither Ruth nor Orpah had children with their husbands, and within 10 years their husbands and father-in-law all died. This left the girls alone with their mother-in-law, Naomi.

Because all the men in Naomi's family had died, the land in Bethlehem that once belonged to Elimelech and her sons now belonged to Elimelech's male relatives. When Naomi heard that the famine in Judah had ended, she decided to return to her hometown. Without family, money or property, Naomi hoped her relatives would take care of her.

Ruth and Orpah started on the journey to Bethlehem with their mother-in-law. But Naomi tried to convince them to stay in Moab, their hometown, where they had a better chance of marrying new husbands and having children. After some discussion, Orpah agreed and returned to Moab, but Ruth insisted on staying with Naomi.

It was harvest time in Bethlehem, and news of Ruth's devotion to Naomi spread across Bethlehem. So Boaz – one of Naomi's relatives and a wealthy landowner – made sure that Ruth and Naomi could gather plenty of leftover barley from his fields. As Ruth went to the fields every day to pick up the food, Boaz watched and admired her effort.

> **Girl Talk!**
>
> *It gets crazy on school mornings at my house. But before we go, Mom makes us stop, hold hands and pray. I feel very calm after that and it helps me all day.*
>
> —Keesha M.
> age 10
> Colorado

The law then said that when a man died, his brother or nearest relative must marry the man's widow. Naomi noticed Boaz's admiration and compassion for Ruth, and she urged Ruth to remind Boaz of his obligation to marry her. Boaz knew of a closer relative, but when that man gave away his right to marry Ruth, Boaz and Ruth were free to marry. Boaz also arranged for Elimelech's property to be returned to Naomi.

After Ruth and Boaz married, they had a son named Obed. Obed's grandson was King David of Israel, an ancestor of Jesus.

Because of her selfless devotion and loyalty to widowed Naomi, Ruth was rewarded with a new family, and Naomi lived the rest of her life surrounded by love.

❋ Read all about Ruth and Naomi in the Book of Ruth.

Naomi and Ruth took care of each other. Without Naomi, Ruth would not have married Boaz and given birth to Obed. Without Ruth, Naomi would have spent the rest of her life depending on other people for a home, food and money.

1. Why did God put Naomi and Ruth together?

_____

_____

2. How do you and Mom take care of each other?

_____

_____

3. How has God taken care of you and Mom?

_____

_____

Read
....
✳ Psalm 100

Pray
....

Dear God, thank You for being You. Thank You for Mom. Please bless us, keep us close to each other and close to You. Amen.

 Do It!

Prayer Chain

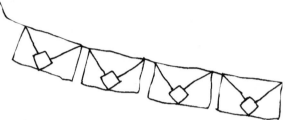

String together folded-paper envelopes, add your prayers and make a "prayer chain."

 What You Need

❋ Origami papers, about 6-inch square

❋ String or dental floss, 2½ feet

 What to Do

1. Make an envelope by folding the paper as shown.

Step 1: Lay paper at a diagonal.

Step 2: Fold bottom point up to meet top point.

Step 3: Fold right point toward center, then fold left point toward center.

Step 4: Fold tip of left point backward.

Step 5: Pull tip back so point faces you. Push in on tip so it forms a diamond shape.

Step 6: Fold down top and fit tip into diamond-shaped slot.

2. Make 10 more envelopes, so you have 11 total.

3. Write each fact from this book (the chapter titles) on the outside flap of an envelope—one fact per envelope. (Example: the first envelope should say "She's Mom," the second can say, "Mom Cares About Me," and so on.)

4. Open each flap, and write the Scripture reference at the beginning of each chapter. (Example: the first one will say "1 John 4:11," the second one will say "John 3:16," and so on.)

5. Fold each flap over the string, starting with the first envelope and moving left to right.

6. Close the flap into the envelope "latch." (You can fasten it closed with a small piece of tape if needed.)

7. Hang up your Prayer Chain (along a wall in your room, for example). Hang it low enough that you can reach it.

8. Starting with the next chapter in this book, you'll write prayers to put in each envelope.

The View

In each chapter you will see this section with questions to ask Mom. (And there are some for Mom to ask you!) You can ask them  as part of a formal interview—as if you were a talk show host or roving reporter—or whenever you're curious or want a conversation starter.

Why should you want to interview Mom? One reason is it's one great way for you two to spend some time together and get to know each other better. Another reason is that your answers can become a permanent record of your life right now—like a letter or a home video.

Think you don't know how to interview anyone, not even your own mother? Think again. You've done an interview if you:

❋ Met someone (say, in your class or youth group) and talked with him or her for the first time

❋ Collected information from someone for a story in the school newspaper or yearbook

❋ Asked questions before deciding to buy something, like a computer game or tickets to a concert

❋ Played a game that asks players to answer questions about themselves

❋ Tried to figure out what to get someone for Christmas or a birthday

❋ Talked to parents about babysitting their kids

Sure-fire tips for doing a sensational interview

1. **Collect your tools**: something to write on, something to write with, and maybe a tape recorder if you want to listen instead of write.

2. **Set up a time and place** with Mom. Choose a quiet place. Not good times: when Mom's driving in heavy traffic, just before bed or while you're getting ready for school. Good times: after dinner, on the weekend.

3. **Get your interview questions ready.** Ask yourself, *What do I really want to know about Mom that I don't already know?* Many times when you do an interview, the person to whom you're asking the questions (the "interviewee") will say something that makes you think of a different question. It's fine to ask questions that aren't on your list.

4. **Pray.** Before you go to the interview place, say a prayer. Ask God to bless the time you are about to share together. Ask Him to open your hearts to each other.

Important: The key to a great interview is to ask great questions. Period. A great interviewer doesn't interrupt the person she's interviewing, and she doesn't give her own opinion. When the interview is over, remember to thank her.

Here's the first set of questions. You can always think of your own to ask, too.

For you to ask Mom

What did you want to be when you grew up? Why?

Did you ever want to run away from home? Did you do it?

What are you thankful for?

What are the three best things about being a mom?

What do you think heaven is like?

For Mom to ask you

What do you want to be when you grow up? Why?

Describe your idea of a "perfect mom." Is she someone you know?

What will you name your kids?

Which day in your life would you like to live over again?

What is your favorite holiday? Why?

✔ Checkpoint

Here's where you take stock of your thoughts and feelings so far and plan your strategy before moving to the next topic.

What did you learn about Mom or your relationship with her?

_____

_____

What did you learn about your relationship with God?

_____

_____

How do you know that God is God? (Read Exodus 6:7)

_____

_____

What do you hope to get from reading this book?

_____

_____

Write a prayer about this fact. Your prayer can be a praise, a request or an "I'm really confused and I need You to help." Then put the prayer in the first envelope of your prayer chain.

Psst! Some moms raise their children the same way their parents raised them. Other moms try to raise their children by doing the exact opposite of their parents. Ask Mom how her style is the same and different as her parents' style. Knowing this can help you understand why she treats you the way she does.

For God so loved the world that he gave his one and only Son, that whoever believes in him shall not perish but have eternal life.

~ John 3:16

FACT 2

Mom Cares About Me.

Mom Cares About Me

👆 I know because...

❋ She asks tons of questions about my friends, school and activities.

❋ She cooks my meals, does my laundry and shows me how to save and spend my money.

❋ She tells me to redo my homework when it's wrong or messy.

❋ She prays for me every day.

❋ She loves me all the time (even if she doesn't always like everything I do!).

Until you were born, there was no one in the world just like you. In that moment when you were born, you filled a place in your family, a seat at the table and a tender spot in Mom's heart.

It's no accident that when Mom first met you—by giving birth to you, adopting you, marrying your dad, or in any other way—she got knocked off her feet with love for you. (If you've ever heard the term "head over heels in love," this is what it means.) This feeling began in her the moment she first saw you. Without having to think about it, she moved out of the spotlight and placed you there instead.

God put that special love in her to make sure she'd protect you and take care of you no matter what. Mom loves you so much that she would gladly die for you in a split second if she had to.

Jesus loves you that much, too. He did die for you, so that you could have a close, loving relationship with God forever.

In The Beginning: Yours!

Just like no one else in this world is just like you, how you were born into this world was unique and special. Here is one way you might have been born:

Mom began to feel crampy pains in her abdomen, and she knew it was time for you to be born. She or your dad called her doctor and said, "It's time for the baby!" Then they all met at the hospital.

On my birthday my mom always tells me the story of when I was born. I know my story by heart, but I still like to hear my mother tell it.

—ANDI P.
AGE 10
NORTH DAKOTA

Mom changed into a hospital gown, and the nurses checked her pulse, her temperature and then her body to make sure you were doing okay inside her.

After many hours of hard work, you were born. Mom and Dad felt so happy and relieved because you were finally here, and they could see you, touch you, smell you, hear you and–of course–kiss you.

A nurse rubbed you with a towel and gave you to Mom to hold. Mom kissed your face– peeking from a warm blanket–and said, "I'm so glad you're here. We waited such a long time for you." At that moment, love like she'd never felt before flooded her heart.

In the days and weeks after you were born, as Mom spent more time feeding and rocking you, changing your diapers and clothes and watching you sleep, she realized her love for you had nothing to do with what you did or didn't do. It had nothing to do with what you looked like or what you wore, whether you smiled or screamed, or whether you fussed or cooed.

She loved you even when you spit up, dirtied your diaper and cried all night. She loved you just because you were hers and because you were you.

She might even have understood for the first time how God could love her in just the same way. Knowing that, she loved and trusted Him more deeply. Mom grew closer to God just by your being born. How awesome is that?!

FAQs

mom:
I need
to talk
Love, Chloe

Q: My mom's really busy. Sometimes I need her attention but I don't want to bother her.

A: Your mom cares about you even when she's busy. She has so much to do as a mom. If she also has a job outside the family, her job takes up even more time and energy. Tell her you want some time with her. Send her a pager message, an email, a voice mail, or slip a note in her briefcase or lunch bag if you have to.

Q: How can I show my mom I care about her?

A: You know your mom best, but here are some ideas to make her smile (or maybe even faint!):

* ✳ Do your chores and homework without being reminded.
* ✳ Let her have some conversation time with Dad without being interrupted.
* ✳ Make her a simple breakfast on Saturday morning.
* ✳ Ask "Mom, can I get you anything?" while you're up from the table.
* ✳ Before asking her for help, see if you can do it on your own (like looking up the spelling of a word in the dictionary).

Q: I don't know how to tell if my mom cares about me.

A: Moms are often very tired and stressed out because there's never enough time to get everything done. Your mom might assume that because she buys groceries and makes meals for you, takes care of you when you're sick, signs you up for activities and then drives you to them, makes sure you're hanging with the right friends, and nags you to do your chores, finish your homework on time and sit up straight at the table, you must KNOW she cares about you. But sometimes that's not enough, and you want to hear the words. So ask her, "Mom, do you care about me?" She'll say, "Of course I care about you–I'm your mother." What she might not tell you is, next to her relationship with God, the most precious thing in her life is you. And you can be 200 percent certain of that.

God Cares About Me

Do you know any of these girls?

Tracy has an unmarried mom.

Kana was adopted.

Angela lives with her mom every other week because her parents are divorced.

Carmen lives with both parents.

Brittany calls her stepmother "Mom."

Heather only sees her mom twice a week because her mom is in a hospital recovering from drug addiction.

Christina is being raised by her grandparents because her mom died when Christina was two.

Although each girl has a different situation and a different kind of relationship with her mom, God cares about each one equally. No matter what your family looks like, God cares about you.

He cares when you're having a fabulous day and when your day is crummy. He cares that you're stressing over your history test tomorrow and about your ongoing battle with your sister over whose turn it is to shower first. He cares that you're heartbroken because you didn't make the team, or because your best friend is spending more time with a new friend and less time with you.

God wanted you to be born. He planned families to care about each other, because it's the best way for you to stay safe, healthy, protected and loved. He commands Mom (and Dad) to take care of you and teach you all about Him. Then, when you grow up, you'll know how to take care of your own children.

Girl Talk!

My mother is a nurse and sometimes doesn't get home until after I'm asleep. She puts notes on my pillow when she comes home so I can read them when I wake up. She writes things like "I love you" and "sweet dreams" and "you look like an angel."

—HaNNaH S.
aGE 11
KaNSaS

Mum's The Word!

In Afrikaans: Ma
In Ainu: Hapo
In Arabic: Om

Profile
Rebekah and Her Mom

Rebekah's name means: captivating

Born in: Nahor, a town in Aram Naharaim (now Iraq)

Her mother: unknown name

Her father: Bethuel, an Aramaean

Brother: Laban

Husband: Isaac (one of Abraham's sons)

Children: Esau and Jacob

Grandma: Milcah

Granduncle: Abraham (Rebekah's grandfather, Nahor, was his brother)

Rebekah lived in the town of Nahor with her mom, dad and brother, Laban. One evening Rebekah went to the town's spring, carrying a water jar on her shoulder. It was one of Rebekah's chores to fetch the family's water every day. She went in the evening because the air was cooler that time of day.

After Rebekah filled her jar that evening, a man she'd never seen ran over and asked her for some water from her jar. She poured water into her hands so he could drink. Then she brought water for the man's camels.

The man, who was Abraham's chief servant, took a gold nose ring and two gold bracelets from his pack and offered them to Rebekah. He asked who she was and if there was room in her family's house for him to stay for the night.

"Sure," she said, "we have room for you, your camels and your men," and she told him who she was.

The man then praised God for sending Rebekah, a relative of his master, to him.

"What's going on?" Rebekah asked.

"My master is Abraham," he explained. "His son, Isaac, is ready to marry. God told my master to find him a wife here in his home country. Just before you came to the spring, I prayed to God that the young woman who offered water to me and my camels would be the one Isaac should marry. And then you offered us water."

When the servant told the story to Rebekah's father and brother, and they realized Rebekah was truly God's answer to the man's prayer, they said Rebekah could marry Isaac.

Abraham's servant wanted to return to Canaan right away, but Rebekah's mom and brother said, "Let her stay here 10 days or so; then you may go."

When I'm sick, Mom lets me sleep in her bed and watch TV in her room. I love her bed because it's huge. I wish I could sleep in there when I'm not sick, too!

—Noelle H.
age 9
Minnesota

Because the grownups couldn't agree, they asked Rebekah what she wanted to do. She said she'd go to marry Isaac, and all her family blessed her before she left for her new life in Canaan.

✳ Read more about Rebekah in Genesis 24 and Genesis 27.

Time Out!

1. Why do you think Rebekah's mom wanted her to wait awhile before she went to Canaan?

_____

_____

_____

2. Rebekah probably never saw her mom again after she left. If you were Rebekah and you stayed for 10 days, what

would you want to do with Mom during that time? What would you say to her, and what would she say to you?

_____

_____

3. Write five things that Mom has done or said in the past week that have shown you she cares about you:

_____

_____

4. What are five things you could do for Mom to show you care about her?

_____

_____

5. Write five things that God has done in the past week that has shown you He cares about you:

_____

_____

 Read
✳ John 17:24-26

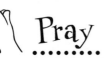 Pray

Dear God, thank You for Your awesome love, which Mom and I can share with each other. Help us to show that love to each other better and more often. Amen.

➤ Do It! ◀

"I Am What I Am" Game

Everyone has several identities.
For example, Jesus called Himself:

The vine

Son of Man

A bridegroom

The Bread of Life

The good shepherd

The Alpha and Omega

The way, the truth and the life

Living water

Just as we call ourselves by different names, people see us in different ways. For example, here are some names people use for Jesus:

Emmanuel	King of Kings	Lord of Lords
Lamb of God	Light of the world	Son of God
Son of David	Hosanna	Savior
Messiah	The Great I Am	

Other than "mom," how many different identities does Mom have? How many different ones do you have? Play "I Am What I Am" with her and find out. You can play this game anywhere. You don't need any equipment or game pieces. Here's how you play:

1. Start by saying, "I am a…" and say an identity that starts with "A." For example, "I am an apple eater."

2. Then Mom should say, "You are an apple eater," repeating what you said and adding, "and I am a…" with an identity that starts with a "B." For example, "You are an apple eater and I am a Bible study leader."

3. Then you should repeat what you've both said so far and add a "C" identity. The goal is to remember everyone's different identities. Whoever misses has to start the game again with "A."

4. If you get all the way to "Z," play the game backwards (from Z to A).

5. Another way to play this game is to name the other person's identities. For example, you could say, "You are Aunt Ann's sister," and Mom could say, "I am Aunt Ann's sister and you are a badminton champ," and so on.

The View
Time for an interview (or a casual chat).

For you to ask Mom

Tell me about when I was born and what you thought when you first saw me.

What about me makes you happy?

What about me makes you worry?

How or why did you choose my name?

What other names did you think about naming me?

For Mom to ask you

When you're feeling sad, what foods do you like to eat?

What's your favorite time of day? Why?

With whom do you wish you could spend more time?

What scares you?

What are the best and worst things about being your age?

✓ Checkpoint

What did you learn about Mom or your relationship with her?

_____

_____

What did you learn about your relationship with God?

_____

_____

Do you know Mom cares about you? How can you be sure, or how can you find out?

_____

_____

How does Mom know you care about her?

_____

_____

How can you be sure God cares about you? (There are many ways to be sure, and here's one to read: Romans 8:32)

_____

_____

Write a prayer about this fact. Then tuck your prayer into the second envelope of your prayer chain.

Psst! When you were a baby and slept most of the time, Mom checked to see if you were still breathing several times a day and night. She might have even jiggled your bassinet to make you stir. It was a rare time when she was happy to hear you cry!

You may ask me for anything in my name, and I will do it.
~ John 14:14

FACT 3

i Can Talk
with Mom.

i Can Talk with Mom

i know because...

* She asks me how my day went.

* She turns off the radio in the car so we can talk.

* When I need to tell her something, she doesn't say, "Not now, honey."

* She doesn't criticize when I tell her my problems.

Do you sometimes feel that Mom is talking to you in code, as if only she knows what she means and you are left to figure it out? Or has Mom ever asked you to explain something you said or did because she couldn't understand it?

Because God made each of us unique, we all have our own particular ways of communicating how we feel and what we want. If we say or do something and the other person gets it, then there are no problems. But when we just think they understand us and they really don't, there can be trouble. You can probably think of a time when you said or did something that Mom took to mean something entirely different from what you meant.

Cracking the Code

There are many different ways to communicate. Of course, we can TELL people how we feel just by saying so. But have you ever known when people were angry or happy or sad, even if they didn't tell you with words? Think about how a person feels when she:

* slouches her shoulders
* jiggles her foot
* arches her eyebrows
* waves her hands in the air wildly
* smiles with only her mouth
* smiles with her mouth and her eyes

All of these physical clues are "body language" and they tell you about a person's mood just as much as what she or he says. (Another clue to people's moods are the tones of voice they use.) If you've ever seen pantomimes–also called "mimes"–you probably understood what they were saying just by watching their body movements and facial expressions.

You can also find out about people by how they treat other people. For example, what do these actions say about these people:

✳ Mom gives you a hug when you're sad. (love)

✳ A child is crying in the middle of a busy street. (fear)

✳ Your neighbor takes care of stray dogs. (compassion, kindness)

✳ Your sister slams the bedroom door. (anger)

✳ Your friend gives you her favorite bracelet. (generosity and affection)

Even when people talk, they can say one thing and mean something very different. For example, check out the girl at right.

At first, it sounds as though she really liked doing the project, doesn't it? But, if you look closely

I CAN'T TELL YOU HOW MUCH I LIKED DOING THAT SCIENCE PROJECT

at the words, you see it could mean she thought exactly the opposite about the project. She honestly couldn't tell you how much she liked it, because she didn't like it at all!

Mom has her own code language. As her daughter, you may know more about Mom's codes than you think. Still, some of her codes might puzzle or confuse you.

* Does Mom move her body or speak in codes? What do they mean?

_____

_____

_____

I wish my mom would listen more. One time I even said, "Mom, you're not listening to me, are you?" and she said, "You caught me." She said she was sorry but she still does it!
—Nicole B. age 11 Maine

* Which of her codes don't you understand?

_____

_____

* How do you know when she's:

Happy? _____

Angry? _____

Sad? _____

Tired? _____

Worried? _____

Frustrated? _____

Hungry? _____

Nervous or Anxious? _____

Needing a hug? _____

Q: My mom always gets mad when I roll my eyes and sigh. I can't help it–it's how I express myself! Then she says, "If you're going to act like a child, I'll treat you like one," and we end up fighting.

A: Back when you were in preschool or kindergarten, your teachers said, "Use your words, not your fists" to express your feelings. That becomes more important as you grow up, because talking about your feelings shows others that you have control over your emotions instead of the other way around. Rolling your eyes and sighing means you don't agree with what you're being told, but it's not a mature way to express your feelings. When you do it to your mom she feels like you don't respect her. She reacts to that, which gets the conversation off-track, and you both stomp off or stop talking to each other. How good is that? Think of some phrases you could use instead of the body language, such as: "I don't agree. Can we talk about it without fighting?" or "I don't think that's fair, and this is why…" or "Can I do it after dinner/on Saturday/after school instead?" You'll shock your mom with the difference in your response. And the more you show her you can act maturely, the less she'll treat you like a child.

Q: I can tell when my mom is angry because she doesn't talk much. I'd almost rather hear her yell than be so quiet, because it scares me if I don't know what she's thinking or feeling. How can I get her to talk?

A: Your mom might be one of those people who likes to mull over what's bothering her before she says something. She might be afraid she'll say the wrong thing and make matters worse. Or, she might not understand exactly why she's angry and so she doesn't have the words to express her feelings. Chances are, if she knew her quietness scared you, she'd stop doing it. So try to get her to talk about what's bothering her. You could say, "Mom, you're being awfully quiet, and I know you're angry. Will you please talk to me about it? I'd rather hear your words than know you're angry and not know why." Ask God to help you. He wants you to live harmoniously with each other and not bear grudges.

Q: My problem is that my mother talks too much. It's not that she's always telling me what to do--she just talks a lot about everything. I love my mother, but her talking frustrates me so much that I don't feel like telling her anything. How can I tell her without hurting her feelings?

A: You can be loving and respectful and still let your mom know how you're feeling. Why does your mother talk so much? Is she lonely? Do you think she feels like no one pays any attention to her? Maybe she's uncomfortable with silence, or maybe it's just a life-long habit. Once you try to figure out why she does it, compassion will overcome your frustration and irritation. When her talking starts to bother you again, you could say, "Mother, I love you. Can I tell you about my day now?" Or, "Mother, right now I just want to be quiet with you. Could we just be quiet for five minutes?" Or, ask her why she talks so much. This is a sure-fire way to have a deep and meaningful conversation in which you BOTH can take part.

i Can Talk With God

Some people think there's a special language they have to use when they pray to God. They get so nervous about using the right words that they don't pray very often.

Mum's The Word!

In Danish: Mama
In Dutch: Mamma
In E-mail: DM
("dear mother")

You would probably never say this to Mom:

"Dearest Mother, humbly I request thee to convey to your lowly female offspring a refreshing quaff of liquid sustenance from the bovine species."

You'd be searching the dictionary all day just to ask: "Mom, can I have a glass of milk?"

The same is true when you pray to God, because praying to Him is talking to Him and then listening for His reply. That's all it is.

Some people don't like to pray because they're so mad or sad, or even happy, that they can't find the right words to express how they feel.

Imagine you actually went to visit God at His house.

"My dear daughter!" He says and holds out His arms. You run to Him and He gives you a big hug and you feel how strong and protective and loving He is. You feel better already.

"Sit down," He says. "I'm so happy you came to see me. Tell me what's going on."

"But don't You already know?" you ask.

"Of course, but I want to hear it from you."

"God," you say, struggling for just the right words, "Thou hast delivered me from manifold quandaries. Verily..."

"Huh?" God says.

"I'm trying to tell you what's wrong."

God leans closer to you. "Just use whatever words you can. I'm listening to your heart, not your words."

"But my heart's all mixed up."

"Not to me. Now, tell me what's bothering you."

You smile, relieved and start over. "Well, see, there's this girl and she's like…"

When you pray, it doesn't matter if you don't have fancy words, or if they're in the wrong order, or even if some words are missing. God knows exactly what's in your heart when you pray to Him. Making the effort to go to Him with your prayer is what matters.

The Servant Girl

Lived in: Israel, and then Aram after she was captured

Daughter of: Parents in Israel

Naaman was a commander in the Aramean army. Although he worked hard to become a valiant soldier, he had leprosy, a terrible skin disease. There was no cure for leprosy in those days. No amount of money, power, success or fame could cure it.

In Bible times, it was illegal for people with leprosy to touch other people or even stand near them. Other people avoided "lepers," as they were called, because they were terrified that they, too, would catch the disease. (Maybe you can think of some diseases we have today that frighten people in similar ways.) So as powerful and successful as Naaman was, he could not conquer leprosy.

Although Aram, Naaman's country, had a peace treaty with Israel at the time, the two countries still fought small battles with each other along their border. During one of these battles Naaman's soldiers captured a young girl from Israel, and she became a servant to Naaman's wife.

This girl was taken from her family and turned into a servant. She

was forced against her will to do whatever her mistress wanted. Most people would become angry, bitter and even vengeful toward their captors, but this girl loved and honored God. So she tried to make the best of a bad situation.

The servant girl knew about Naaman's leprosy. She also knew of Elisha, God's prophet. She knew that God's power could heal people. The servant girl was sure that Elisha could cure Naaman's leprosy. So instead of keeping this very important and special knowledge to herself (which many people in her situation would have done), she said to her mistress, "I know a prophet of God who could cure your husband's leprosy. He should go to Samaria where the prophet is living."

Naaman's wife gave this information to her husband, and Naaman went with his servants to see the King of Israel. He took a letter of introduction and explanation from the King of Aram, and several thousand dollars worth of silver as payment for the cure. But in spite of the king's wealth and power, he could do nothing to heal Naaman.

When Elisha heard about Naaman, he sent a messenger to tell Naaman how to be cured. Naaman was to wash himself seven times in the Jordan River. Naaman couldn't believe this was the cure he'd been hoping for! He'd expected Elisha to snap his fingers or wave his hand to cure him. But Elisha knew that he had no powers to heal. Those powers were all God's, and Naaman had to understand clearly that God—not Elisha—would heal his leprosy. If Naaman wanted to be cured, he must obey God no matter how crazy it might sound.

Naaman finally did as he was told, and after he washed himself seven times in the Jordan River, his skin became clear and smooth again. He was cured! He returned to Elisha and said, "I know now that there is no other god but yours, the God of Israel." Naaman became a believer in God. And it was all because a servant girl chose to set aside her circumstances and share God's love with someone who was hurting.

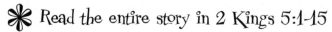 Read the entire story in 2 Kings 5:1-15

Time Out!

1. If you were the servant girl, would you have told your boss about a cure? Why or why not?

_____

_____

2. In addition to being cured of leprosy, what greater thing happened to Naaman because the servant girl talked to his wife?

_____

_____

3. Are you keeping secrets from Mom that she should know? Why don't you tell her?

_____

_____

4. What good things could happen if you choose to tell Mom rather than keep secrets?

_____

_____

Read

✳ Romans 8:26-27

Pray

The Lord's Prayer. (If you don't know it, ask Mom, or read Matthew 6:9-13). Think about each phrase as you say it.

➤ Do It! ◀

Code Secrets

Here's a way to give Mom a message that only the two of you understand.

☞ ## What You Need

✳ thin plastic beading cord

✳ letter beads

✳ decorative beads

✳ scissors

🌀 What to Do

1. Decide what you want your bracelet to say, and how you'll make a code. Here are some ideas:

   - Word scramble. Jumble up the letters of your message.

   - Acronym. An acronym is a word (or words) made up of the first letter of each word. For example, "ILY" is "I Love You" as an acronym.

   - A different language. For example, "Je t'aime" is "I love you" in French, and "Itsumo" means "always" in Japanese.

- A code you create. For example, use the letter that comes right after the real letter of your message. For example, J'N ZPVST says I'M YOURS.
- Spell the message backward.

2. Go to the craft store and pick your beads. Remember to choose decorative beads without letters, too.

3. Put the cord around Mom's wrist, making sure she can slip it over her hand. Then add 2½ inches to that measurement (for tying and trimming the cord).

4. Measure the cord to that length. (Measure it unstretched.) Then cut it to that length.

5. Tie a knot in one end of the cord.

6. String some regular beads onto the cord, then string your letter beads. Finish with more regular beads. (You could also mix the letter and regular beads!)

7. Tie a knot at the other end. Put the bracelet on Mom's wrist. She should be able to slip it off easily.

8. When the fit is just right, tie the ends together and trim them.

My mom is pretty cool when it comes to talking about stuff. If she thinks I'm being too quiet about something, she tickles me and then I always laugh. Sometimes I wish she wouldn't treat me so much like a kid but I like it when she pays attention to me.

—Delia H.
age 11
California

The View

Time for an interview (or a casual chat).

For you to ask Mom

If you could say something to someone who's dead, who would it be and what would you say?

What was your favorite book when you were my age?

What has been the happiest day of your life, and why?

How does God talk to you?

What prayers has He answered, and how did He answer them?

For Mom to ask you

If you found out your best friend was doing something she (or he) knew was wrong or harmful, would you tell her (or him)?

Would you also tell a grownup? Who?

Do you know someone who's hard to get along with? What can you do about it?

When you are with your friends, are you talkative, quiet, a leader or a follower?

If you could ask someone from the Bible a question, who would it be and what would you ask?

 Checkpoint

What did you learn about Mom or your relationship with her?

_____

_____

What did you learn about your relationship with God?

_____

_____

Can you talk with Mom? How can you be sure, or how can you find out?

_____

_____

How does Mom know she can talk with you?

_____

_____

How can you be sure you can talk to God? (Read Matthew 21:22)

_____

_____

Write a prayer about knowing you can talk to God. Tuck your prayer into the third envelope of your prayer chain.

Psst! Mom checks in on you one last time before going to bed to make sure you're okay. Then she kisses you or touches your forehead and says "I love you. God bless you. Sweet dreams." She does this even if you two had a terrible day together.

But store up for yourselves treasures in heaven, where moth and rust do not destroy, and where thieves do not break in and steal.

~ Matthew 6:30

FACT 4

Mom Is Proud of Me.

Mom Is Proud of Me

i know because...

❋ She puts pictures of me all over the house.

❋ She tells people about my accomplishments.

❋ She shows Grandma and Grandpa my artwork.

❋ She gets this funny look on her face when I'm nice to other people.

❋ She says, "I'm so proud of my girl."

The first time Mom looked into your eyes, touched you and smelled your skin, a strong and special bond formed between you. From that moment on, anything you did or said made her heart swell with pride, because you were her child.

You smiled, and she beamed. You rolled over onto your back, and she applauded. You said "ah-goo!" and she called all her family to tell them you said your first word. You fed yourself with a spoon (and got most of it in your hair and on the floor), and she was certain you had the ability of a neurosurgeon or fine artist. Everything you did from the day you were born swelled her heart until it hurt.

You're not a baby anymore, but Mom is still very proud of you, whether she tells you often or not much at all. She might show how proud she is by displaying your artwork around the house, sending an email to her sister about your  latest field hockey save, posting reviews of your stage performances on the family web site, or telling her friends that you read to your younger brother at night. When she hears you leading a prayer or humming a hymn or praise song in the back seat, her eyes fill with tears of pride and love.

You also know the things that don't make her proud. You know what they are, but here are some examples:

* You fibbed about where you went after school one day.

* You glanced at someone else's exam when you weren't sure of the answers.

* You hinted to your brother that you'd tell on him if he didn't lend you his favorite sweatshirt.

* You peeked in your sister's diary.

* You "borrowed" money from Mom's wallet, or took just one little pack of gum from the drugstore.

* You called your brother something you've been taught not to say.

* You didn't speak up about something you knew was right because you were scared that your friends wouldn't like you anymore.

You know these things wouldn't make Mom proud because she has taught you what's right and wrong. It's easy to convince yourself that these things aren't wrong, but you know they are wrong because they give you the guilts and shames–not good feelings to have! You should be able to brush the guilts and shames aside and feel okay about yourself. But you can't because they create a barrier between you and Mom, and between you and God. This is just where the enemy (you know which enemy) wants you to be. The guilts and shames rob you of the joy and peace that only honesty and goodness can bring!

You also know the cure for the guilts and shames: confess your sin, ask for and receive

forgiveness and do your best to resist doing it again. And that's an attitude that will make Mom truly proud!

FAQs

Q: Last year I got caught shoplifting and was punished for it. My mom wasn't proud of me at all, and she still brings up what happened. I feel so bad about what I did, and I'll never do it again. How can I make her proud of me again?

A: Daughters (and sons) want more than anything to please their parents and make them proud. Your mom probably doesn't hold a grudge against you for something you did a long time ago. She was disappointed in your behavior then (and would be if you did it again), and perhaps worries that you'll do it again. But she's extremely proud of the times you make good choices. Try asking her to tell you about those times, and remind her that you've changed since last year.

Q: Sometimes I hear my mom talking about me to her friends. Most of the time she talks about things I did that she was proud of. But sometimes she says things I don't like. What can I do?

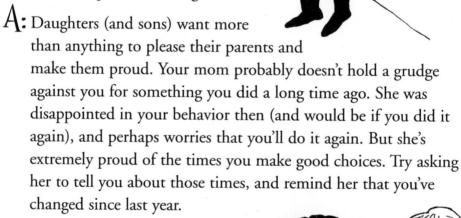

A: It feels great when you hear your mom telling other people about what you did well. It tells you she noticed your accomplishments (great or small). But it hurts when you hear her talk about the other things—the things with which you struggle. It's bad enough that your mom isn't proud of it, but you don't want the entire world to feel the same way—especially when they hear only one side of the story. Your mom might not realize she's hurting your feelings, so you need to tell her. Encourage her to keep saying the good things. Then you can be proud of your mom for her accomplishment!

God Is Proud of Me

It feels so good when people—especially those you love—praise you for positive things you've done. (On the other hand, it feels terrible when they notice the not-so-positive things!) You know that getting praise or rewards from other people isn't why you do them. When Jesus talked to His disciples about giving, he said we should do it in secret, so that no one knows about it. What matters is God knows you've done it, and He'll reward you for it.

A girl I know says how much she likes me and then tells lies about me behind my back. Mom said I should talk to the girl instead of doing the same thing to her. Mom told me gossip is evil, and the Bible says Christians are supposed to turn from their evil ways.

—Amy F.
age 13
Iowa

In his letter to the Philippians, Paul told the people of the church at Philippi to be careful of what they're proud of. Being proud of the way they looked was the wrong focus. The right focus was thinking, acting and talking in ways that pleased God.

Just like back then, being proud of your clothes, hair and nails, or what kind of house or neighborhood you live in, is the wrong focus. There's nothing wrong with having these things, but paying too much attention to them instead of acting the way God wants gets you off track really fast.

You know when God is proud of you, because you can feel His praise glowing in your heart.

Profile

Miriam and Jochebed

Miriam's name means: rebellious (Hebrew)

Jochebed's name means: God's glory (Hebrew)

Both born in: Egypt

Miriam's father/Jochebed's husband: Amram

Brothers/sons: Moses and Aaron

You probably know how the story goes. God had promised the Israelites that they would have lots of children who would grow up and have lots of children, and so on. This made the king of Egypt (also called "Pharaoh" or "Ramses the Great") very nervous. If the Israelites kept having babies, they would soon be able to take over the country, he thought. That would mean he would be out of a job, and the Israelite people would have power over the Egyptian people, instead of the other way around.

Girl Talk!

Every Christmas my mom writes a letter to me and hangs it on the Christmas tree. She writes a Bible verse and then something she likes about me. She's been doing this since I was born.

—Brianna T.
age 9
California

So, Pharaoh forced the Israelite people to be slaves for the Egyptian people. They worked many hours each day doing the hardest work in Egypt, such as building entire cities and pumping water from the Nile River into the fields where they plowed, planted and harvested crops. And they didn't get paid for all that work.

Despite the long, hard work they did for no money, the Israelite women continued to have many babies (according to God's plan). Pharaoh's plan wasn't working! So the Pharaoh ordered the Egyptian people to drown every baby Hebrew boy.

Around this time, a Hebrew woman gave birth to a baby boy.

(She later named him Moses – and he later led the Israelites out of Egypt to freedom, but that's another story.)

Moses' mom kept him out of sight as long as possible. But when he was three months old, she knew she couldn't hide him much longer.

She had an idea. She put her baby boy in a basket made of papyrus and hid him in the reeds along the edge of the Nile River. The baby's older sister, Miriam, stood along the river to watch and make sure nothing bad happened to him.

Mum's The Word!

In Chinese: Mama
In Chinook (Eskimo): Mama
In Czech: Maminka

Nearby, Pharaoh's daughter, the Princess of Egypt, decided to take a bath in that same river. When she saw the basket, she asked her maid, "What's that over there? Bring it here."

When the princess opened the basket, she saw the baby boy and heard him crying, and her heart filled with love. Just then, Miriam came out of her hiding place.

"That baby's starving," Miriam said. "He wants milk."

"You think?" said the princess.

"I can find a Hebrew woman to nurse him."

"Yes, hurry!"

Miriam knew just the right woman to nurse the baby: her mom! God protected Moses and saved his life through the acts of his mom and sister. The Pharaoh's daughter raised this son of a Hebrew mom and dad as an Egyptian prince!

 Read more about Miriam and Jochebed in Exodus.

The Miriam Show

Miriam might not have known that her mom was proud of her unless she and her mom talked about it. What if Miriam had her own talk show and her mom was a guest? By talking to her mom, Miriam would find out how proud her mom really was. This might be how the episode goes:

Miriam: Welcome to the show. Today we're talking with Moses' mom, who just happens to be my mom, too.

Mom: It's great to be here. I can't believe you're all grown up with your own talk show! Do you have your own dressing room?

Miriam: [*clears her throat*] Well, let's start. What was it like back then, just before Moses was born?

Mom: [*shakes her head*] It was a scary time. We had to work 24/7 for no pay. It was back-breaking work building cities, breaking up rocks for roads and walls and digging irrigation trenches for the crops and drinking water. We plowed the dirt, sowed the seeds and picked and harvested all the crops. We fainted in the hot sun. Many people died while they worked.

Miriam: So, tell us about when Moses was born.

Mom: He was a beautiful baby—just like you. He was so sweet, too. It was a blessing he was so quiet, because the neighbors would certainly have turned him over to Pharaoh's soldiers if he'd cried. It broke my heart to have to give him up. Putting him in the river was the last thing I wanted to do. But what else could I do? I loved him too much to let Pharaoh kill him. I'd seen lots of little boys taken from our neighbors and relatives, and then killed. I wasn't going to let that happen, and neither was God.

Miriam: Tell us about God in all that.

Mom: I couldn't protect Moses from Pharaoh, so I gave him over to God. I said, "He's Your boy, not mine." And with your help, God protected Moses in that basket.

Miriam: Pharaoh's daughter could have taken him out of the basket and thrown him in the river, just like her father ordered.

Mom: That was also part of God's plan. She kept him, loved him and later adopted him. [*pauses and gazes at Miriam*]

Miriam: What?

Mom: I was just remembering…

Miriam: [*looking desperately into the camera*] Yes? [*whispers*] Don't zone on me.

Mom: …how you were right there with Moses, watching out for him. You were such a loving sister.

Miriam: Of course. He was my baby brother.

Mom: I wonder what would have happened to him if you hadn't been there that day. He might have drowned, or I might never have seen him again. I've always been so proud of you, Miriam.

Miriam: But Moses was the one who led our people out of slavery. I always thought he was your favorite.

Mom: Moses got all the attention, but without you he'd never have gotten famous. Now look at you – you have your own show, your own dressing room…

Miriam: Mom…

Mom: Are you picking up after yourself? Putting the milk back in the fridge? Hanging up your wet towels?

Miriam: [Turning to the camera.] Thank you, Mother! That's it for today, folks.

Mom: …Drinking enough water? Exercising?…

[*theme music grows and fades*]

Time Out!

1. If you were Jochebed, what qualities in Miriam would make you proud of her?

_____

_____

2. If you were Miriam, what would you admire about Jochebed?

_____

_____

3. What qualities in you make Mom proud?

_____

_____

4. What do you admire about Mom?

_____

_____

5. What are you not proud of and would you like to change? (Remember, you can always ask God to change them in you!)

_____

_____

Read

✳ Philippians 3:1-11

Pray

Dear God, thank You for giving me gifts and talents I can use to help other people. Help me to be proud of the right things, even when Mom doesn't notice. Remind me to tell Mom I'm proud to be her daughter. Amen.

~→ Do It! ←~

Desert Planter

You might not expect to find many flowers growing in the desert. In fact, many colorful wildflowers and other beautiful plants grow in deserts. You can make a planter for Mom and plant wildflower seeds in it. Your planter will be a reminder that beauty even can come from difficult situations.

☞ What You Need

* an empty can
* yarn, crafting cord or twine
* double-sided tape
* white glue
* stars, gems, shells, foam shapes, ribbon or buttons
* potting soil
* pebbles
* package of mixed wildflower seeds

 What to Do

To Get the Planter Ready

1. Wash the can and remove the label. (A 24-oz beef stew can works well, but any size is fine)

2. Ask an adult to make 15 small drainage holes in the bottom of the can by driving a nail through the bottom.

3. Have an adult check for any sharp edges around the can's inside rim. These can be removed by sanding, pounding with a hammer or covering with clear sealing tape or glue.

4. Wrap the double-sided tape around the outside of the can at the top and bottom rims. Wrap two more strips around the middle. Then place strips from top to bottom around the can, about 1½ inches apart.

5. Press the starting end of the yarn near the bottom rim of the can, and wind the yarn around the can, working upward. Turn the can with one hand, and guide the yarn with the other. Every inch up, push the strands of yarn downward to close up any gaps.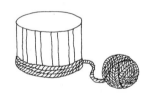

6. When you reach the top, dot glue along the top strand to keep it in place. Cut the yarn, and dot glue on the end to keep it in place. Use a bag clip or clothespin to hold the end in place until the glue dries (about 5 minutes).

7. Add ribbon, stars, buttons, shells, ribbons or other decorations to finish the planter. For example, create a desert look by placing blue ribbon along the bottom (for water) and top (for sky) of the can. Use double-sided tape to fasten it to the planter. Then add stars, a moon, a sun, a cactus, a camel, a palm tree and brown beads for rocks.

8. Now that your planter is ready, it's time to plant the seeds!

To Plant the Wildflower Seeds

1. Place the pebbles about ½-inch deep in the bottom of the planter.

2. Fill the planter with potting soil.

3. Follow the instructions on the seed packet for planting and growing the wildflowers.

The View

Time for an interview (or a casual chat).

For you to ask Mom

What personal or professional goals did you set and accomplish?

What helped you accomplish them?

What are you proud of about me?

What do you wish Mom had told you about yourself but didn't?

If you were a guest on a talk show, what would you talk about?

For Mom to ask you

What has been the most difficult thing to learn?

What are some good things that people have said about you?

If you were a character in a book, who would that be?

What three things do you like best about being a daughter?

What three things would you like me to change?

✔ Checkpoint

What did you learn about Mom or your relationship with her?

_____

_____

_____

What did you learn about your relationship with God?

_____

_____

How do you know Mom is proud of you, or how can you find out?

_____

_____

How can you be sure God is pleased with you? (Read Colossians 3:23)

_____

_____

Write a prayer about knowing God is pleased with you. Then tuck your prayer into the fourth envelope of your prayer chain.

Psst! Even though Mom's a grown-up, she still wants to feel appreciated by the people she loves. When you were a little girl, you often told her she looked pretty or smelled nice, and said "I love you" and "Thanks" and gave her lots of hugs. She might be missing that overflow of love from you now. If you'd like to really make her day shine, compliment her (tell her she's awesome or she looks great), thank her unexpectedly, or hug her for no particular reason. Try this every day for a week and see what happens. You'll probably notice that she treats you more kindly and lovingly. You both win!

For God, who said, "Let light shine out of darkness," made his light shine in our hearts to give us the light of the knowledge of the glory of God in the face of Christ.

~ 2 Corinthians 4:6

FACT 5

Mom Doesn't Expect Me to Be Perfect.

Mom Doesn't Expect Me to Be Perfect

i know because...

❋ She says, "Just do your best."

❋ She says we're all works in progress.

❋ I've seen her make mistakes, too.

❋ She says God uses my imperfections for good.

"Tuck in your shirt." "Sit up straight." "Smile and shake hands." "Don't leave trash all over the car/kitchen/your bedroom." "Practice until you've got it right." And so on and so on. Sound familiar?

It might seem like Mom only talks when she wants to criticize you, correct you, and try to make you perfect. Believe it or not, Mom doesn't expect you to be perfect, but she does hope you will become the best you can be. And she knows it's her job to help you get there.

Read on to find out how Becca, Kara and their moms help them to do their best.

Kara's Lie

Kara clicked the front door shut and tiptoed into her room.

"That you, Kara?" her mom called from the kitchen.

Kara took out her English notebook and turned it face down on her desk. In it was her project with a huge, red "C+" on the top.

"It's me," Kara answered. She punched her pillow before falling onto her bed.

"Come on out and tell me about your day."

"I...don't feel good, Mom. I just want to stay here awhile."

Her mom came into the bedroom. "Did you catch my cold?"

Kara shook her head. "I just don't feel good."

She looked at Kara's desk. "Oh, you got your project back today. How did you do?"

"Okay," Kara said and tried to smile. "I got an A." Kara knew God didn't want her to lie—especially to her mother—but she didn't want to disappoint Mom.

Her mom looked intently at Kara and then smiled. "Great, honey! I know how hard you worked on it, even though you were so sick with the flu then. Can I see it?"

"I left it at school," Kara said. She felt worse about lying a second time.

"Okay," Mom said and stood up. "Let me know if you need anything."

"Thanks, Mom," Kara said. Now her stomach really felt sick.

Did it sound like Mom would have been upset if Kara told her the truth about her grade?

_____

_____

How would you change the ending to this story?

_____

_____

From Becca's Diary

(She gave us permission to peek!)

October 4: Mom and I started cleaning out the garage today. We probably won't finish 'til next July. So much of it was stuff I had thrown in there because I ran out of space in my bedroom. Mom said, "You should have thrown that out a year ago." She was pretty annoyed by the time we finished.

October 11: Mr. Merino gave the part in the musical to Rosa Hernandez. She definitely did a better job than me in auditions, but I still really wanted that part. So it was hard to think of anything else today. I tried all day not to cry. Mom and I worked more in the garage after school. Almost done. We found some of my first-grade homework in a box. My writing was really messy then. (See-Mom keeps things, too!)

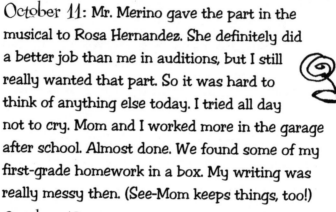

October 18: When we were in the garage yesterday, Mom found my old metal sand bucket in a box. Mom said that Aunt Donna gave it to me when I was two. I remember filling it with water and making castles with it. Mom said I carried it like a purse. She said I went from her to Dad begging for pennies for my purse. She said I put tadpoles in it, too. And wore it on my head! (But not with tadpoles in it-yuck!) Mom wanted to throw it out. It's full of holes, the sides and bottom are torn and the handle is broken. But I wanted to save it. "Please let me keep it," I said and put it in the Keep pile. She

said I had too many things in that pile already. Besides, that bucket is good for nothing now. So then I said OK and put it in the Trash pile.

October 25: Mr. Merino asked me if I wanted to take the part of someone in the crowd. All I get to say is "Look out for the car!" to Rosa, but I also walk around on stage. And I can work on some props, so I said yes. It will be fun, I guess. I changed my mind about my bucket. Even though it was broken, I wanted to keep it. But the trash truck came today, and the bucket was gone. Mom said I was "very sentimental" and gave me a kiss. I think she's sentimental for keeping my old homework.

November 1: Rosa and I were talking at lunch today. She was crying because she's really scared about doing the musical. She said, "I never studied so many lines. I don't think I can do it." I told her I'd practice with her, and she's coming over next week.

November 8: Rosa and I practiced her lines after school. It was so funny to play all the other parts! Mom gave her some ideas for making her lines easier to remember (like pretending she's walking through different rooms in her house, and the lines of her part go in different rooms). Rosa said she felt weird that I was helping her, because she knew I wanted her part. But I told her it was OK. It doesn't matter anymore, because I think she's going to do a great job. Mom and I prayed for her tonight.

November 15: The musical opened tonight, and Rosa remembered all her lines. She did great! She got a bouquet of roses at the end, but she gave them to me afterward, because she said that practicing with me helped her so much. When we got home, Mom told me to shut my eyes. She took my hand and walked me to my bedroom. "Now open them," she said. I couldn't believe it-my old sand bucket was on my dresser, only it was a lampshade! Mom took it out of the Trash pile after I went to bed that night and put some pretty fabric on it. It's so cool because the light shines through all the cracks and holes and makes awesome shapes on the walls. Mom said the bucket reminded her of me when I helped Rosa. She said she was so proud of me because I let Jesus shine His love through me to help Rosa.

Bye, Diary!

Becca

What did Becca expect from herself?

_____

_____

Did her mom expect the same thing?

_____

_____

What did Mom notice about Becca that Becca didn't?

_____

_____

Q: My dad left my mom a few years ago, and I live with my mom. They still argue when they see each other, and it makes me feel terrible, like I'm bad. I can't talk to my friends about it because they all have perfect families. What can I do?

A: It is not your fault that your parents cannot get along. You are not bad or evil or less valuable than your friends. However, you are in danger of developing a poor image of yourself, which could affect you for the rest of your life unless you talk to someone who can help. Because your mom and dad do not see how they're hurting you, it's up to you to take charge. Talk to one of them about seeing a counselor who can help all of you learn to communicate in positive ways. If your parents can't or won't go, talk to an adult you trust, such as your aunt or uncle, a grandparent, a school counselor, a teacher, coach, Sunday school teacher, or your pastor or youth leader. Talk to someone. Don't keep it inside you. And keep praying to God to remind you that He loves you and wants to help.

I wish my mom wasn't so tired all the time. I think she needs to get more exercise or not go to work.

—Kathryn D.
age 11
California

Q: My mom DOES want me to be perfect. My clothes and hair have to be just right, my homework has to be 150 percent, I have to play the piano without making any mistakes—and even eat perfectly. But I don't do everything the way she wants, so I feel like she's always disappointed in me. I try, but I don't do any better. What's wrong with me?

A: Your mom is probably urging you to get into the habit of doing your very best now because she knows that when you grow up there will be tons of people competing with you. Lots of people are smart, well-dressed, musically talented and have polished social manners. She probably wants you to stand out so that you can be successful and make a good living. The problem is that no one can be perfect. Someone can be the best and most celebrated pianist in the world, for example, but eventually that honor will be taken away by someone who plays even better. Someone else can be the most brilliant architect in the country, but there will always be someone more creative. Also, that pianist or that architect can't possibly be the best at everything she does—maybe she's clumsy on the tennis court, can't balance her checkbook or doesn't know how to be a good friend. When you live in a world where people compete with each other to be the most successful or celebrated, it's hard to remember that in God's eyes these qualities are not important. In fact, they are foolish things to pursue. God wants us to strive for the kind of perfection that Christ showed. And the only way to become that

My mom used to cuss all the time but she's been trying to stop since she became a Christian. To help her quit, every time she cusses she puts a malted milk ball in a certain jar (she hates them!). Then on Saturdays she has to eat all the balls in the jar!
—Lilly M.
age 11
Mississippi

kind of person is to keep your relationship with God alive 24/7.
When you read the Bible, pray and stay involved with your
church, Christ's perfection takes hold of your life
and shows itself in the things you think, say and
do. The rest of the world—your friends, teachers,
classmates, maybe even your parents—may not
notice or understand these Christ-like attitudes
and behaviors. But God does, and ultimately that's
what really matters. So talk to your mom about
what she expects from you, and why. Ask her if

Mum's The Word!

In Farsi: Mamma
In Gaelic: Mathair
In German: Mutter

she wants you to meet her exact standards in everything, or if
trying to do your best is more important. Ask her if you can
choose what's really important and worth going the extra mile.
For example, does your room have to be always completely neat,
or can you let that slide a bit and concentrate your time and
energy on practicing for the piano recital? Talking with her,
instead of resenting or being afraid of her, is showing the kind of
perfect, Christ-like behavior that pleases God.

God Doesn't Expect Me to Be Perfect, Just Faithful

"If God made me," you wonder,
"why didn't He make me perfect?
Why do I have crooked teeth,
thin hair, a bad temper. Why am I
a klutz? And why do I keep doing
things I'm not supposed to?"

Many adults, including Mom,
have probably told you that looks
don't matter. But you know that's not always true—a girl's hair, skin,
features and clothing all affect the way other people think of her at
first. Yet our opinions about people's appearances usually change when
we get to know them.

To test this out, think about your friends, girls and guys. The reasons you chose your friends probably had nothing to do with the way they look. You like them because they're fun, loving and caring. Once you get to know someone, you realize that your opinion of her physical looks is based on her character, instead of the other way around. A pretty girl who gossips is suddenly not pretty anymore. On the other hand, an average-looking guy who helps you with your homework can be really cute in your eyes.

God doesn't care about your physical flaws or how many mistakes you've made. He has known you since before you were born. He loves you with all your faults and flaws (just like Mom does). God doesn't expect you to be perfect—that's impossible for any person. But He does want you to let Him guide you in every aspect of your life, because His plan for you is to become more like Jesus. Ask Him to help, and He will!

King David wrote: "I praise you because I am fearfully and wonderfully made; your works are wonderful" (Psalm 139:14). Flaws, faults and all, you are one of God's most magnificent creations!

Profile Leah

Her name means: tired (because of her "weak eyes"? –see Genesis 29:17)

Born in: Haran

Mother: unknown

Father: Laban, an Aramaean

Sister: Rachel

Husband: Jacob (Rebekah and Isaac's younger son)

Children: six sons and one daughter

Leah had a younger sister named Rachel. Laban, the girls' father, tricked Jacob (Rebekah's son) into marrying Leah. But Jacob was in love with Rachel and he married her, too. (In those days, a man could have many wives at the same time.)

Girl Talk!

My mom and dad got divorced, and my brother and I live with my mom. We go to our dad's two times a month. I like that my mom doesn't disrespect my dad. They used to fight a lot, but they don't so much now. I think my mom's happier now, but I wish we could all live together again but with no fighting.

—Yumi M.
age 11
Massachusetts

Because Jacob loved Rachel, Leah never felt that Jacob loved her. But God blessed Leah with seven children: sons Reuben, Simeon, Levi, Judah, Issachar and Zebulun, and a daughter, Dinah. All six sons became leaders of the tribes of Israel.

Leah's youngest son, Judah, was an ancestor of David, who became King David—who was an ancestor of Jesus. Even though Jacob didn't love Leah, God loved her and blessed her by making Jesus her descendent.

God can always use us for His work. When you feel unloved, know that God loves you and has a special plan for your life.

 Read more about Leah in Genesis 29.

Time Out!

1. In the story, what happened that probably made Leah feel sad and unwanted?

_____

_____

2. How did God use Leah's situation for good?

_____

_____

3. What about you or your life is painful or disappointing?

_____

_____

4. Has God used that situation in a good way, or can you think of a way He might use it for good?

_____

_____

5. Can Mom help you with this problem? How?

_____

_____

Read
✳ Matthew 5:14-16

Pray

Dear God, thank You for loving me even though I'm not perfect. Please keep guiding and teaching me. Please keep shining Your love through my flaws so that other people can see You in my heart. Amen.

 Do It!

Shining Lights

This activity will remind you of God's light shining in you.

 What You Need

* glass baby food or jelly jar
* various colors of tissue paper
* scissors
* white glue
* small paintbrush
* shallow bowl
* votive candle or tea light

 What to Do

1. Remove the label from the jar. Wash and dry the jar thoroughly.

2. Cut several colors of tissue paper into small shapes.

3. Pour the glue into a shallow bowl and mix in some water to thin it. Keep adding water until the mixture is like cream.

4. Hold a piece of paper on the outside of the jar, and brush the glue mixture over it until it is stuck to the jar.

5. Glue more pieces. You can overlap them to create different colors, or place them side by side. Cover the entire jar, but not the rim. (The paper could catch fire if it's inside the jar.)

6. Place the candle inside, and ask an adult to light it.

7. Enjoy the beautiful colors!

The View

Time for an interview (or a casual chat).

For you to ask Mom

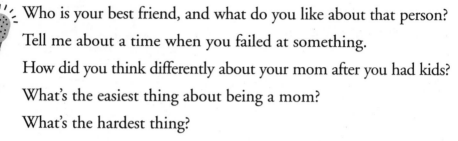

Who is your best friend, and what do you like about that person?

Tell me about a time when you failed at something.

How did you think differently about your mom after you had kids?

What's the easiest thing about being a mom?

What's the hardest thing?

For Mom to ask you

When you're a mom, what will you do differently than I do?

What's one problem you'd like to trade with another person?

If you had an identical twin what good things would you say about her? What would get on your nerves about her?

If an alien came to dinner at our house, what five things would you say about our family? About Jesus?

(If you have sisters or brothers) Do you ever feel like I expect more from you than from your sister or brother? Why?

 Checkpoint

What did you learn about Mom or your relationship with her?

_____

_____

What did you learn about your relationship with God?

_____

_____

Do you know Mom doesn't expect you to be perfect? How can you be sure, or how can you find out?

_____

_____

How does Mom know you don't expect her to be perfect?

_____

_____

How can you be sure God accepts you, flaws and all? (Read Romans 8:28-30)

_____

_____

Write a prayer about being sure God accepts you. Then tuck your prayer into the fifth envelope of your prayer chain.

Psst! Mom didn't go looking for flaws the first time she saw you. Instead, she checked you all over to figure out if you were healthy. Then she realized you were the most breathtaking creature she had ever seen. She still does!

Do not let your hearts be troubled. Trust in God; trust also in me.

~ John 14:1

Mom Can Trust Me
(and I can trust her).

Mom Can Trust Me
(and I can trust her)

I know because...

✳ I tell her where I'm going and with whom.

✳ She answers my questions honestly.

✳ She gives me a little freedom, and that's exciting.

✳ She never snoops in my room or my diary.

One way Mom can tell you're growing up is that she can trust you. That means you do what you say you'll do, and you do what's right. It means your room will be picked up when it's supposed to be. It means you'll be with whom you've said you would. It means you'll be home when Mom expects you to be.

The more you show Mom she can trust you, the more privileges she will give you as you get older. Read Shawna's email below to see how her mom learned to trust her more.

From: Shawna Davidson
Sent: Saturday, August 7
         8:47 PM
To: Tara Browne
Subject: Tonight

Tara, you still up? You won't believe what happened tonight. Jessica and I went to the carnival up at church. Mom told me I could go. *But* she gave me money to buy some bread on the way home. *Big* but, because I forgot. I didn't really forget, I spent it on a game. (I won a goldfish! He's swimming on my dresser.) The thing is, I knew I spent the

bread money, but I told Mom I forgot she asked me to buy the bread. I felt bad about lying, but I was scared of what she would say. When I got home, she was so mad she could hardly talk and sent me to my room.
Write later, Shawna.

Why was Shawna's mom so angry?

_____

What should her mom do, and why?

_____

Will that be fair?

_____

If you were Tara, what would you write to Shawna?

_____

There's more to this story!

From: Shawna Davidson
Sent: Saturday, August 7
         9:30 PM
To: Tara Browne
Subject: Tonight

Tara, you will never in a million years guess what happened. I can hardly believe it. Right after I emailed you Mom knocked on the door. I thought she was going to ground me for life. But she said, "I was thinking about what I could do to punish you. Then I remembered something that happened when I was in high school. My mother told me to buy milk on my way home from a fair, but I didn't buy it because I already spent all her money. She was so angry I didn't think I'd live to see the next day." The she said, "I trusted you and you let me down. That's the worst part. We need bread for tomorrow's breakfast. I wanted the bread so I could make French toast for you"–which, BTW, is my favorite thing to eat–"so, you didn't just spend my money, but you made me wonder if I can trust you." I told her I was sorry. She told me I can't go anywhere for two weeks and I have to do extra chores. I feel so awful that I broke her trust. I'm going to make sure she can trust me from now on. I'm glad she didn't take away email privileges.

Love, Shawna.

Q: Mom doesn't trust me. She's always looking in my diary and my email. But I haven't done anything wrong! It makes me not trust her either. I don't want to write what I really think because I don't know what she'll do with it.

A: It does feel like an invasion of privacy when someone looks into your private thoughts. You have a right to keep those things private. Remember, though, that your mom wants you to be safe. With all there is to threaten your safety, she's probably not being a snoop as much as she is trying to protect you. What if some person who wants to do you harm is sending you email and pretending he or she is someone your age? What if you're doing something, like drugs or drinking, and writing about it in your diary? What if you're spending too much time with one boy instead of having a healthy balance of many friends and activities? She wants to know these things and has decided that looking into your private places is a good

My mom is really honest so I trust her to tell the truth. She said that whenever she tried to lie her face got red and her voice got shaky so she gave up trying!

—Lisa P.
age 10
California

way to find out. If none of these things is happening to you–and nothing else that you know your mom wouldn't approve of–then tell her so. Let her know she can trust you by what you say, do, wear and with whom you hang out. Give her reasons why she can trust you. Ask her if she can agree not to snoop as long as you give her no reason to do so. Once you can agree on that, your trust in her will also be restored.

Q: I wish my mom trusted me more. She's always asking "Who are you talking to on the phone?" or "Why are you wearing that?" or "Who was waving to you?" It's embarrassing. She even came to my youth group meetings a few times –and stayed there the whole time–before she let me go by myself. A river rafting trip is coming up with my youth group, and I bet she'll sign up as a chaperone. I feel like a prisoner in my own life! I'm really careful about who I talk to on the Web, in school and out in public. What can I do to make her trust me?

A: It sounds like your mom is taking very good care of you. It also sounds like you're learning to take care of yourself well. By doing her best to protect you, she's accidentally giving you the message that she doesn't trust you. She probably trusts YOU, but not the world. She knows the world holds harm for young girls (and boys). You won't like hearing this, but you need to put up with her protectiveness until you're a few years older. If you try to understand her motives, you might be able to accept her attitude during this time. She protects

In Ancient Greek: Mhvthr
In Modern Greek: Mama
In Hawaiian: Makuahinem
In Ancient Hebrew: ~a 'em

you because she loves you. By the way, having your mom come along on the youth trip might be a fabulous experience for you both! Before you go, talk about what you each expect from the other. If it will embarrass you for her to be too much of a "mother," ask her to try curb those tendencies around your friends. Tell her ahead of time what kinds of things will embarrass you and ask her what kinds of things would make her unhappy. Decide where you'll sleep and agree on what you can do.

Q: My mother criticizes just about everything I do, including how I do my chores. She doesn't trust me to do them the right way, which is HER way. I don't want to do everything her way. Doesn't it matter just that they get done? I feel like she watches me and waits for me to make a mistake so she can correct me. I feel like she'll even correct me if I talk to her because I'm not using the right grammar. What can I do?

A: You probably feel like you want to either scream or go into your room and never come out. Your mother is trying to teach you, but she has trouble letting you develop your own style of doing things. For example, her style might be to wash the dishes as she cooks, and yours might be to clean everything after cooking. In most cases, there isn't one right way to do things, so whether you cook and clean her way or yours, the food gets cooked and the dishes get washed. Even in serving God, not everyone will serve Him in the same way, and that's His plan. He makes us all a little different so that we can

Girl Talk!

Mom says she trusts me to make the right choices, but sometimes I want her to help me. I'm not old enough to decide some things.

—Kayla D.
age 13
Minnesota

offer ourselves in our own, unique ways. One girl may show His love by babysitting in the nursery, while another might show His love by praying for her friends, but both are serving God. Ask your mother if you could do your chores while she's in another room, at work, out of the house or just not watching. Assure her that you'll do them on time. After awhile, she'll see that you can be trusted to get things done on time and will appreciate your unique style of doing them. In time, she will also see that you can be trusted to do other things well. Be careful, though, to stay open to your mom's teaching and mentoring, which help you learn and improve. Your mother is just one of hundreds of people you'll meet in life who will tell you things that can help you become a better person, but you have to listen to them first.

I Can Trust God, Too

Whether you're 1 or 101, you are God's child. He wants you, as a Christian, to trust Him with your worries and problems. God is always in control of everything, even when you feel like things are completely out of control in your life, your family, at school, at church or in the world.

Are you:

❀ being bullied?

❀ worried about being chosen for a team?

❀ wondering how you'll ever pass the next science test?

❀ brokenhearted because your best friend moved?

❀ suffering from an illness?

❀ sad because someone you loved died?

❀ scared or ashamed because someone is abusing you?

❀ worried about your safety at school or home?

❀ frustrated that you never seem to get what you want?

It may be hard to trust God with these problems because they're so big and hard for you to solve. He wants you to have faith in Him and in how you fit into His kingdom. Read the story below to see how your life fits into God's "big picture."

You come home from school and Mom hands you an invitation that had come in that day's mail. It says:

Come to my house next Saturday and bring this puzzle piece.

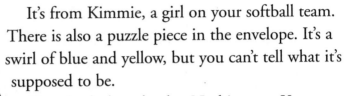

It's from Kimmie, a girl on your softball team. There is also a puzzle piece in the envelope. It's a swirl of blue and yellow, but you can't tell what it's supposed to be.

You check the calendar. Nothing yet. You could say you'll go to the party, but decide to wait. Something better might come up. You put the invitation and puzzle piece back into the envelope.

On Saturday you're still not sure if you'll go. The phone rings. It's Kimmie.

"You gotta come," she says.

"I don't know yet." Sometimes commitment is so difficult.

"Please come. I really want you there."

"Well, okay," you say as you calculate how long it will take you first to finish cleaning your room as Mom had asked.

"Great!" she says. "Don't forget the puzzle piece."

What's so important about a puzzle piece, you wonder, but you put it in your pocket so you don't forget it.

Kimmie greets you at the door of her house. "It wouldn't have been the same without you," she says. "Now, close your eyes and keep them shut."

Kimmie leads you by the hand. "Now open them."

On the floor is the biggest jigsaw puzzle you've ever seen.

Someone had blown up a photo of you sliding into home to win the championship. Your teammates jump up from behind couches, chairs and bookcases. "Surprise!" they yell.

Kimmie shows you where your piece fits. When you fit it into the hole, the picture is complete.

"It wouldn't have been the same without your piece!" says Kimmie, and you're so glad you showed up at the party.

Your Christian life is like a puzzle piece that fits into something much larger. You don't know where the piece fits or what part of the whole it is – and you probably never will. Sometimes you might even be unsure about whether your piece fits at all. But God, who created the puzzle, knows and He asks you to take your puzzle piece with you. That's where trusting in God comes in.

I want to trust my mom, but a lot of times she says she's going to do something and then she doesn't.
—Maya C.
aGe 11
CoNNecticut

A single puzzle piece by itself serves no purpose. But when it's put into the whole puzzle, the result is awesome and powerful. When you trust God to do what He commands, you get to be part of His exciting plans. Having faith in Him is all He asks of us.

 Mary

Her name means: bitter (Hebrew)

Lived in: Bethlehem, Egypt, Nazareth

Mom of: Jesus

Wife of: Joseph of Nazareth

Related to: Elizabeth, mother of John the Baptist (Jesus' cousin)

Mary was just a teenager when she became engaged to marry Joseph. During that time, an angel named Gabriel came to Mary with greetings from God. (Can you imagine how terrified she must have been to see an angel and hear him talk to her about God?)

Gabriel told her to calm down because he had good news: she would become pregnant with a son who would be called the "Son of the Most High" and would rule with God forever over heaven and earth.

Mary wondered how this could possibly happen–how could she become pregnant when she and Joseph weren't even married yet? Gabriel explained that this would happen through the Holy Spirit and reminded her that God can do anything. After all, He is God.

Although still terrified–and probably feeling confused–she told Gabriel she'd do whatever God wanted her to. After all, she was His servant. God can also use you in wonderful ways when you trust Him.

✳ Read much more about Mary in: Matthew 1-2 and Luke 1-2.

  **Time Out!** 1. Why did Mary agree to do what Gabriel told her?

_____

_____

2. What might have happened if Mary had refused to go along with the plan?

_____

_____

3. Why is doing what God wants always a good choice, even if you don't understand why?

_____

_____

4. In what ways have you, and do you, trust Mom?

_____

_____

5. In what ways does she trust you?

_____

_____

 Read
✳ Hebrews 11:1-16

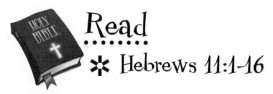 Pray

Dear God, help me to show Mom that she can trust me to do what's right, especially when she's not around. Amen.

~→ Do It! ←~

Time in a Bottle

Here's a fun project to do alone or with Mom: a time capsule! A time capsule contains items that describe you and your life right now. Months or years from now you can open it and see what was going on.

☞ What You Need

✳ a sturdy plastic container of any shape, about the size of a large shoebox. You can decorate it with stickers or paints.

✳ duct tape

✳ items to put in the time capsule. Here are some ideas:

- **A letter to yourself.** Write about your typical day, friends, hobbies, dreams, goals, favorites, or how you imagine your life will be in 5 years.
- **A Scripture verse.** When you open the time capsule you'll see how God has worked His promise into your life.
- The day's **newspaper** or a current **magazine**
- Pages from a **fashion magazine** (it's fun to look at old fashions and hairstyles)
- The **movie and TV pages,** and **car and real estate ads,** from the newspaper
- This week's **church bulletin**   • Your **handprint**, or hand outline
- **Pictures** of you and Mom   • A lock of your **hair**
- A piece of your **artwork**   • A **picture of your pet**
- A **wrapper** from your favorite food or candy bar
- A **tape recording** of you, or you and Mom

 What to Do

1. Put the items in your time capsule, making sure not to crush them. Don't put anything in plastic sandwich bags, because the condensed moisture will ruin the contents.

2. Write today's date, your name and Mom's name on a piece of paper. Put the paper on top of all the items.

3. Close the lid of the time capsule. Then seal the seams with duct tape to make the time capsule airtight.

4. Decide when you'll open it. Five years is good, but a year is fine. Then tightly tape a note on the outside of the time capsule that says: "Do not open until (the date you decided on)."

5. Put the time capsule in a dry place such as a closet or attic. You can even store it in the fridge or freezer. But don't bury it because the items can decompose more quickly if they're underground. Also, you might forget where it's buried. If you move you could forget to dig it up!

I trust Mom with everything. She's so easy to talk to about my problems. I know she'll give me good advice. She's always there for me!

—Mary Alice M.
age 13
New York

What Not to Put in a Time Capsule

- Food or drinks (they can attract bugs and bacteria)
- Lotions or perfumes (they can leak)
- Seeds or plants (although dried flowers are okay)
- Anything flammable or toxic (such as matches or batteries)

Facts About Time Capsules

- Only about 20 percent of all buried time capsules are ever found.
- Many time capsules are planned to be opened long after the people who made them have died.

The View

Time for an interview (or a casual chat).

For you to ask Mom

Do you frequently have the same dream or nightmare (like trying to fly, or taking a test)?

What has been the most embarrassing moment in your life?

When you were growing up, did you feel you could trust your mom? Why or why not?

What three things do you ask God for about me?

Who was your first boyfriend? How old were you? Did your mom and dad like him?

For Mom to ask you

If you had a day completely to yourself, what would you do?

What's the first thing you think about when you wake up?

What's the last thing you think about before you go to sleep?

What will you be doing 10 years from now?

If you had a million dollars, what would you do with it?

 Checkpoint

What did you learn about Mom or your relationship with her?

_____

_____

What did you learn about your relationship with God?

_____

_____

Do you know Mom trusts you? How can you be sure, or how can you find out?

_____

_____

Why, in particular, do you trust Mom?

_____

_____

How can you be sure you can trust that God is in control of your life? (Read Jeremiah 29:11)

_____

_____

Write a prayer about trusting God. Then tuck your prayer into the sixth envelope of your prayer chain.

Psst! When you're older—and perhaps when you have children—things about Mom will make more sense than they do now. When that time comes, you might want to tell her you understand the infinite, overwhelming, invincible, forever, awesome love she feels for you. But, if you don't have the chance to tell her, don't worry because she already knows that someday you will understand. (She experienced the same thing with her mom when you came into her life.)

What has been will be again, what has been done will be done again; there is nothing new under the sun.
~ Ecclesiastes 1:3

Mom Doesn't Know Everything
(but she knows a lot!).

Mom Doesn't Know Everything
(but she knows a lot).

I know because...

* She helps me make right choices.

* She has rules (lots of them) and sticks by them.

* She can drive a car, mow the lawn, work at an office, teach a Bible study and correct my homework.

* She was my age one time...long ago (not so long according to her).

You have many teachers as you go through life: schoolteachers, Sunday school teachers, coaches, Girl Scout leaders, youth group leaders and pastors. And of course, God.

But Mom is one of your most important teachers. Because she's lived longer than you, she's done more and learned more so she can pass all that knowledge and wisdom on to you. Chances are, she learned much of this from her own mother. You might have heard her say "my mother used to tell me this" or "my mother used to do that."

Blazing Trails

Your relationship with Mom as your teacher is like the game Trailblazing. If you've never played Trailblazing, try it when you are camping with a group of people. Here is how you play:

The players divide into two groups. The first group waits at the campsite, and the second group goes into the woods. The group in the woods creates signs and markers out of whatever they find: twigs, rocks, leaves, bark and so on. Each sign gives an instruction, direction or warning, such as "go to the right when the

Girl Talk!

I admire how responsible my mom is, and how organized she is!

—Gayle N.
age 10
California

trail forks" or "waterfall ahead" or "return to camp." As they go along, they draw a map with their signs. When they return to camp, the other group goes out with the map and follows the trail signs. Everyone hopes that group returns!

As a daughter, you are blessed by having a trailblazer in your family–Mom!–who can guide you safely as you grow into an adult. Okay, maybe you've heard your trailblazer say some things more than you'd like, such as "When I was your age…" or "I know these things…I'm your mother." But if you can take a deep breath and really listen, you will learn valuable stuff.

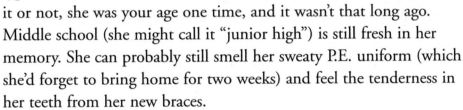

It's so hard to think of Mom being any age except the one she is now. She might talk about things that seem like ancient history to you: LP records, typewriters or ditto machines. But believe it or not, she was your age one time, and it wasn't that long ago. Middle school (she might call it "junior high") is still fresh in her memory. She can probably still smell her sweaty P.E. uniform (which she'd forget to bring home for two weeks) and feel the tenderness in her teeth from her new braces.

Like you, Mom's been on her own life trail. Sometimes she ignored the trail signs and slid over the cliff. Other times she forged her own trail and remembered to leave markers along the way.

Mom can teach you so much, including how to:

* Make your own meals, do your own laundry, manage your money (practical skills you'll need as an adult)
* Treat other people with kindness, compassion and respect, the way Jesus asks
* Honor God
* Resist temptations that will hurt you
* Make wise choices that show you respect yourself

What are some things that Mom tries to teach you?

Q: My mom tells me about doing the right things, but she doesn't always do them. She tells little lies and isn't always honest. Isn't that being two-faced?

A: The saying "do as I say and not as I do" must have been spoken first by parents. It's true that your mom usually knows the right thing to do but doesn't always practice it herself. You learned earlier in this book that your mom isn't perfect–she's human just like you and makes mistakes. She has frustrations, disappointments and bad days, too. Only God is perfect, and if you do what He wants, you're doing what's right. In the meantime, you might gently point out to your mom how she's not doing what she's saying. In this way, you can teach your mom.

Q: Sometimes my mom tells me something that I know isn't true. For instance, she told me I couldn't go swimming after eating because I'd get a cramp and drown. But my friend who's on the swim team said that's not true. I don't want to disrespect my mom, but she isn't always right. How can I tell her that?

A: It's wonderful that you want to show respect for your mom by not talking back to her. Moms often teach their children what they were taught, and in some cases, the facts or current opinions have changed since then and those beliefs are no longer true. (Did you know that people used to think raw tomatoes were poisonous and could only be eaten cooked?) However, just because your friend tells you something different doesn't mean it's true, either. For the swimming example, you should talk to your doctor or school nurse for the current recommendations on swimming right after eating. If you have a question about what your mom says, ask her to give you details that will prove to you that she's right (or not).

Girl Talk!

Mom shares her faith with me by making food for homeless people.

—Emily N.
age 9
California

If you still think she's not right, explain (in a loving and respectful way, of course) why you believe her information is incorrect. For example, you can say, "Mom, I've heard something different about that…" and then explain what you know and where you heard it. It's always best to assume that your mom is correct unless you have a reason to doubt what she says.

Girl Talk!

My mom is amazing and smart. She can do 100 things at the same time!

—Simone P.
age 9
Georgia

And remember that not everything you hear is true, so always check the facts. Also remember that although opinions—and even "facts"—change, the truth of the Bible does not change. If you question something in the Bible that's different from what you've been taught, talk to your mom, youth leaders or pastor. And if someone ever tries to make you do

Mum's The Word!

In Icelandic: Mamma
In French: Mamma
Italian: Mamma

or believe anything that "feels" wrong to you, tell your mom right away. She'll help you figure out the truth.

Q: My mother was 40 years old when I was born. What can she teach me that makes sense today?

A: Just because your mother is older than some other moms you know doesn't mean she can't relate to what concerns you. The basics of life don't change that much from year to year, generation to generation or even century to century. When you read the Bible, you see that people had the same problems then as we do now and they reacted to those situations in the same ways we do now. People have always felt jealous, insecure, angry, scared, rejected, unloved, unappreciated, sick, too fat, too thin and so on. In God's eternal world, the 40 years between you and your mom isn't long at all! To prove it, ask her about when she was your age. For example, ask her to tell you about a bad argument that she had with her best friend, what her mother told her about being kind to people, who in her class was "cool" (or not) and why, and what was her worst bad-hair day. (Many of *The View* questions will also help you know these things about her.) You might realize that you could be having that exact same conversation with one of your girlfriends instead of your mom!

I Can Learn From Jesus

It might feel sometimes that no one in the world–including Mom–could possibly understand you. Maybe you think no one has any idea what you're thinking and feeling. You're even confused about what's going on. Who am I? How do I fit in? Why do people always tell me what I can and can't do? What do people want from me? Why am I happy one minute and sad the next? How can I feel lonely when I have a family and lots of friends?

There is one person who knows exactly what is in your heart. Jesus has experienced it all. Think about this: His mother wasn't married when she became pregnant with Him. Instead of a fine palace, He was born in a stable, where animals eat, sleep and do everything else. Instead of protecting the children, the ruler of Jesus' own homeland killed all the baby boys to make sure that Jesus would die. Instead of many comforts, Jesus as an adult never had money or a home, and He relied on other people to provide Him food, water and clothes. Jesus couldn't even trust all of His friends—one of them had Him arrested and killed for a few coins. He was condemned to die by people who had cheered His arrival in their city just a week before. His own Father wouldn't save Him from the torture of dying in the most horrible, painful way known then. (God knew Jesus had to die so that you could live with Him forever.)

God gave Jesus this difficult life—instead of an easy, carefree one—so Jesus would know what it's like to feel sad, left out, betrayed, lonely, angry and hurt. Because Jesus had such a life, there isn't one question He hasn't asked, or one problem He hasn't faced. There's not one fear, one temptation, one moment of physical or emotional pain or one moment of confusion or insecurity He hasn't experienced. He lived it all and understands it all. You can go to Jesus with anything on your mind and in your heart without being embarrassed or ashamed. You won't be telling Him anything that He doesn't already know.

Jesus said, "I am the way and the truth and the life" (John 14:6). If you look for His trail signs and then follow them, He'll lead you safely home.

Profile

Eunice & Lois

Eunice's name (Timothy's mother) means: noble victory (Greek)

Her husband: unknown name, but he was a Jew

Her son: Timothy, a close coworker of the apostle Paul

Lois' name (his grandmother) means: battle maiden (Greek)

Lived in: Lystra, in Lycaonia, in southern Asia Minor

Timothy went on several missions with the apostle Paul. They traveled to the smaller, isolated Christian churches (when Christianity was still very new) and encouraged the believers.

Timothy was a strong Christian with a deep faith. He already loved Christ when Paul first met him.

Two of the strongest influences on Timothy's childhood were his mother, Eunice, and his grandmother Lois. Paul wrote about them in his second letter to Timothy, when he said "I have been reminded of your sincere faith, which first lived in your grandmother Lois and in your mother Eunice and, I am persuaded, now lives in you also" (2 Timothy 1:5). Timothy, Lois and Eunice all became Christians in Lystra, probably when Paul and his disciple, Barnabas, came to preach.

Eunice and Lois are examples of how moms can help their children love and honor God. Look to Mom to help you know God better, too.

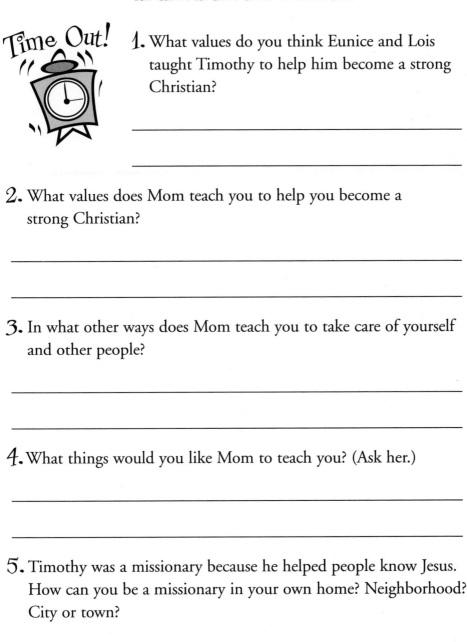

1. What values do you think Eunice and Lois taught Timothy to help him become a strong Christian?

_____

_____

2. What values does Mom teach you to help you become a strong Christian?

_____

_____

3. In what other ways does Mom teach you to take care of yourself and other people?

_____

_____

4. What things would you like Mom to teach you? (Ask her.)

_____

_____

5. Timothy was a missionary because he helped people know Jesus. How can you be a missionary in your own home? Neighborhood? City or town?

_____

_____

 # Read

* Proverbs 2

 # Pray

Dear God, thank You for making Mom my teacher. Please help me remember to watch her and listen to her. Please keep showing Mom the trail signs, too. Amen.

 ## ~→ Do It! ←~

Oven S'mores

Out on the trail and around the campfire, s'mores are the perfect dessert. 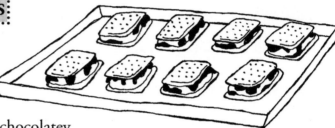 They're warm, gooey, chocolatey and crunchy—all in one bite! Just the thing to eat while you're singing songs, telling stories and getting to know your trail buddies. You can have the same delicious treat at home. Ask Mom to help you make these Oven S'mores.

☞ What You Need

* cookie sheet or shallow baking pan

* 15 plain or honey-flavored graham crackers, broken into squares

* 1 bag of miniature marshmallows or regular-sized marshmallows

* 3 milk chocolate bars (1.55-oz size is best because it's thinner and melts better, but you can use one 7-oz bar or 15 miniature bars)

* aluminum foil

What to Do

1. Always wash your hands before you begin cooking.

2. Heat the oven to 300 degrees.

3. To make cleaning up easy, line the bottom of the cookie sheet with aluminum foil.

4. Place the graham cracker squares in the pan, about one inch apart.

5. Place four miniature marshmallows on each graham cracker. If you're using regular-size marshmallows, cut each one into quarters and place all four on each cracker.

6. Break the chocolate bars into 1-inch pieces (two sections of the bar) and place each piece on top of the marshmallows.

7. Place another graham cracker on top of each s'more.

What I like about my mom is she's an artist and she shows me how to do art like her. She teaches art to me and my friends in the summer. What I wish she would change is she sings too much. In the morning I just want to be quiet but she sings in the kitchen.

**—Malika F.
age 10
Minnesota**

8. Have an adult put the cookie sheet in the oven. Heat the s'mores for about six minutes, or until the marshmallows and chocolate melt.

9. Have an adult take the pan out of the oven. Let them cool about three minutes.

10. Eat—yum!

By the way...

✳ Store any leftovers in the fridge—they're also delicious cold.

✳ Use your creativity—S'mores are extra special with chocolate-flavored graham crackers or different kinds of candy bars.

The View

Time for an interview (or a casual chat).

For you to ask Mom

What was Christmas like when you were my age? What did you do and with whom did you spend it?

What two things do you wish your mom had told you (that you had to find out for yourself)?

What two things did your mom tell you that you still remember?

If Jesus lived in our house for a week, what three things would you want Him to change?

Who was your favorite teacher and why?

For Mom to ask you

What three things don't I know about you that you'd like me to know?

Of all the people you know, whom are you most like? Why?

What three things do you like about me?

What three things don't you like about me?

What event in history would you like to have seen? Why?

Checkpoint

What did you learn about Mom or your relationship with her?

_____

_____

What did you learn about your relationship with God?

_____

_____

How can you be sure Mom is a valuable teacher?

_____

_____

What can Mom learn from you?

_____

_____

How can you be sure that God wants to teach you His ways? (Read Psalm 32:8)

_____

_____

Write a prayer about God's teaching. Then tuck your prayer into the seventh envelope of your prayer chain.

Psst! Mom thinks you're not paying attention when she tries to teach you. So she's astonished when she sees you displaying good character traits! She realizes that maybe she is doing her job as a mom and thanks God for doing His good work in you.

Honor your father and your mother, so that you may live long in the land the Lord your God is giving you.

~ Exodus 20:12

FACT 8

I Can Play by Mom's Rules

(and still have fun!)

1. GO TO BED ON TIME
2. DO HOMEWORK
3. CLEAN UP ROOM
4. WALK DOG
5. CALL IF LATE
6. NO RIDES WITH STRANGERS
7. NO TV ON SCHOOL NIGHTS
8. NO EMAIL AFTER 7PM

i Can Play By Mom's Rules
(and still have fun)

i know because...

❋ I feel safe when I stick to the rules.

❋ She gives me more privileges as I get older.

❋ Sometimes I'm relieved when I have to tell my friends that Mom won't let me do something.

❋ I go online the way she's taught me and still have fun.

Rules, rules. Do this! Stop that! Where are you going and whom are you going with? Brush and floss your teeth every day. Mind your manners. Don't wave your knife. We don't use that word in this house. And on and on.

Life is no fun when you have too many rules to follow. Wouldn't it be great to live without rules and do whatever you wanted whenever you wanted? You wouldn't have to go to school or do homework, wouldn't have to sit quietly in church, you could eat whatever and whenever. You could make up your own rules!

The Science Experiment

What would it be like to do whatever you want whenever you want? Here's one possibility:

Kendra *(calling on her cell phone)*: "Anne? Hello? Can you hear me?"

Anne *(on her bedroom phone)*: "Kendra? What's up? Are you at science camp already? What's all the noise?"

Kendra: "We're here, but the kids have gone insane."

Anne: "Who's screaming?"

Kendra: "Carlos. He just got hit with a water balloon with a rock in it."

Anne: "Where are the parents?"

Kendra: "They didn't come. No teachers, either."

Anne: "Whaaat?"

Kendra: "Mr. Kumar sent us off all by ourselves. He said there were no rules. At first it was awesome, but not anymore."

Anne: "Well, who drove the bus?"

Kendra: "Some guy hardly old enough to have his license. He sat on sleeping bags to see over the steering wheel. I'm scared. It's starting to rain here and the tents are only halfway up. The rest of us are trying to organize teams for supper, but some kids just opened the coolers and are already eating out of them. We won't have any food for the rest of the trip!"

Anne: "It sounds to me like you guys ARE the science experiment!"

It doesn't sound like Kendra's having much fun without rules. In fact, it sounds like having no boundaries is making her feel scared. What could have been a fun and stimulating adventure has turned into a nightmare!

In the book *Little Women* by Louisa May Alcott, the mom allows the four sisters to do whatever they want for a week. At first, the sisters have a blast with no rules or restrictions, but soon they get bored and cranky, and unsure about what to do or how to do it. By the end of the week, they realize that rules have a purpose: to keep everyone safe and healthy—even happy!

You may not agree with all of Mom's rules. Maybe you compare her rules to other parents' rules and think Mom's are unfair, rigid or old-fashioned. But her rules also serve to help you, not punish you. (It's

Girl Talk!

My school has uniforms, but I get money for doing chores and then my mom lets me buy clothes I like. She gives me a dress code, though, like no straps showing. But I still pretty much choose what I want as long as it's in that dress code.

*—Stephanie C.
age 12
Virginia*

when you break the rules that you get punished!) Until you're old enough to live on your own, it's important for you to respect and honor Mom by following her rules.

Q: I lied to my mom about something because I was afraid I'd get in trouble if I told the truth. But it got my friend in trouble instead. I feel terrible about it now, but it seems better to leave things the way they are instead of messing everything up again. What should I do?

A: People often tell lies because they are ashamed to reveal the truth about themselves. Putting the blame on someone else damages his or her reputation. You've seen the pain your action caused. That bad feeling is God reminding you not to lie and urging you to tell the truth. It's so good that you're listening to God and wanting to change the situation. Start by praying and asking God what to do and say. You'll have to suffer the consequences of lying–including perhaps losing your friend–but you'll feel so good that you did what God wants. Knowing you've done what pleases God is worth far more than the convenience of any lie.

Q: My mom tells me to do whatever I feel is right and lets me make most of my own decisions. But sometimes I don't know what is the right thing to do. She says she doesn't want to control me. How can I get her to give me some idea of the best choice?

A: Rules are like the lines on a softball field. When they're there, you know where and how far you can go. You know what happens if you go outside them. They provide a structure within which you can play your game (and have fun, compete and create friendships). Your mom's rules provide a structure within which you can enjoy and find meaning in your life and learn to be a responsible adult. If the lines on your softball field were gone, you'd have no idea how far to run to make a base, if you hit a foul or when a ball is "out." Everyone would get frustrated, and eventually everyone would leave the not-fun game. In the same way, when

your rules at home are loose, ever-changing or nonexistent, you can also become frustrated and even frightened. It's possible that your mom was raised by very strict parents so she decided to never tell her kids what to do. Or maybe it's simply hard for her to set and enforce rules. No one likes to be told what to do and how to do it all the time, but we do crave some boundaries for our behavior. Sit down with your mom and set some rules on which both of you agree. Also set up consequences for you if you don't follow them. Tell her that you'd like her to make more decisions. You may not like her decisions and you may argue about them, but it sounds like you're willing to have her be the boss more often.

> **Girl Talk!**
>
> *My mom always has advice and she helps me stay focused. But I wish she wouldn't say embarrassing things about me.*
>
> —Jodie T.
> age 10
> Nevada

Q: My mom makes me go to bed at the same time as my sister, who's a year younger than me. I think I should get to stay up later since I'm older. How can I get Mom to see things my way?

A: Everyone needs a good night's sleep, and that includes growing girls. If you don't have enough sleep, you won't do well in school,

sports or other activities. You can forget things easily, be really grumpy or make dangerous mistakes in judgment that could harm you. Your mom wants you to be well rested. So, before you say she's not being fair or she's being too strict, think about why you're feeling it's not fair. Is it because you truly think you're going to bed too early or because you don't want to have the same bedtime as your little sister? If you think your bedtime is unreasonably early for your age, explain that to your mom. Ask her if you could stay up an extra hour for a few nights to see if it causes any problems for you the next day (try it on a weekend first!). However, if you are only feeling you don't want the same treatment as your sister, whining about it and saying your mom isn't being fair will not convince her that you're mature enough to handle a change in bedtime. It might even have the opposite effect!

I Can Have Fun as a Christian

Sometimes it feels like being a Christian means you have to learn a lot of rules and then stick to them for the rest of your life. The rules might seem boring and strict at times, especially when they are the exact opposite of what you want to do.

So why does God have all these rules? Because He knows they're good for you! He wants you to enjoy your life as a Christian and be rewarded to the fullest. The reward is living a joyful, peaceful, love-filled life and then spending eternity with Him. But when you don't follow His rules, you can get hurt. Other people can get hurt, too. This isn't God punishing you; it's just what happens when we try to do things our way.

For example, God tells us not to steal. But would it really matter if you took a few dollars from Mom's wallet for a movie? After all, you think, she gives you an allowance–this is just an advance on it. You'll tell her later, you decide, and off you go to the movies.

A few hours later, your little brother falls off his bike and cuts his head. There are no more bandages in the house, and Mom rushes to the store with your bleeding brother. But when she opens her wallet, it's empty, and her checkbook and credit cards are at home. So, your brother has an ugly scar across his forehead for the rest of his life because Mom couldn't bandage the cut properly in time. Plus, when she finds out you took the money, she bans you from going to the movies for months. Everyone loses!

It's a different story when you follow God's rules. Suppose your

Mum's The Word!

In Japanese: Okásan
In Korean: Umma
In Malay: Emak

new neighbor, who's expecting a baby, is told she has to stay in bed until her baby is born. She has a daughter about your age. You remember that God tells us to love our neighbors. So you invite the girl to your house several days after school and on Saturdays to give her mom a break, and you two become best friends. After the baby is born, your friend's mom says, "I don't know what I would have done without you. Our family and close friends live out of state. Because I knew you were keeping my daughter happy, my baby was born perfectly healthy." Everyone wins because you followed God's rules!

Eve

Her name means: Living

Lived in: Garden of Eden
(probably in southern
Iraq)–for a while

Mom of: Cain, Abel, Seth
and others

Wife of: Adam

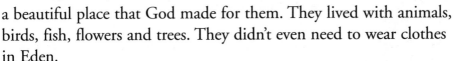

Eve lived with her
husband, Adam, in Eden,
a beautiful place that God made for them. They lived with animals,
birds, fish, flowers and trees. They didn't even need to wear clothes
in Eden.

God had told them they could eat anything they wanted except
the fruit from the Tree of Knowledge of Good and Evil. That fruit was
only for God.

One day, Eve was strolling around, and a snake told her, "Go
ahead and eat from that tree."

"Which tree?" she asked.

"You know which tree I mean. The Tree of Knowledge of Good
and Evil."

"But God told us not to eat that fruit, or we'll die."

"He only told you that because He doesn't want you to be like
Him. If you eat that fruit, you'll know everything, just like Him. You'll
be as wise and powerful as He is. Go ahead, do it."

Eve thought about it. That fruit sure did look tasty. And, why not
get a little help to get smarter? she thought. So, she ate some and she
gave some to Adam.

Suddenly they realized they were naked. They felt ashamed and
embarrassed. They made clothes from fig leaves (which are very large)

and hid from God when he came to Eden to talk with them. They weren't only ashamed that they were naked, they were ashamed that they had disobeyed God! The moment they disobeyed God, their relationship with Him changed. They were so ashamed of what they'd done that they felt awkward spending time with God like they had before.

When God found out what they'd done, he sent them both out of Eden. God told Eve that whenever she gave birth to a child, it would hurt. Eventually, she had three sons: Cain, Abel and Seth.

✳ Read more about Eve in Genesis 2-3.

Time Out! 1. How would Eve's life have been different if she'd done what God told her?

_____

_____

2. List some of Mom's rules and how she disciplines you for not following them:

_____

_____

_____

3. Why do you break her rules?

_____

_____

4. Give an example of how you follow one of the Ten Commandments.

_____

_____

Read
* Deuteronomy 5:6-21

Pray

Dear God, thank You for making boundaries to protect other people and me. Thanks for Mom's rules, too. Help me to make her job easier by following them. Amen.

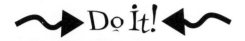

~Do It! ~

Follow this recipe to make a sweet snack for you and Mom.

☞ What You Need

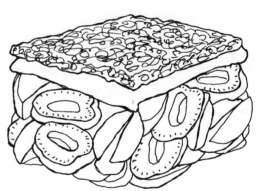

* vanilla-flavored yogurt
* fruit
* knife
* honey (optional)
* mixing bowl
* vanilla-flavored wafer cookies
* plastic storage bag
* rolling pin

◎ What to Do

1. Always wash your hands before you begin cooking.

2. Choose a few different types of fruit that you and Mom like.

3. Ask an adult to help you cut the fruit into bite-sized pieces.

4. Put all the fruit in a mixing bowl, and mix it up.

5. Add 1 or 2 tablespoons of honey, if you like.

6. Place the bowl in the refrigerator for 30 minutes.

7. Meanwhile, put 10 vanilla-flavored wafers in a plastic storage bag and close the bag tightly.

8. With a rolling pin or other object, crush the crackers into crumbs.

9. After 30 minutes, take the fruit out of the fridge, and spoon it into dessert bowls.

10. Spoon yogurt over the fruit, then sprinkle the top with the wafer crumbs.

The View

Time for an interview (or a casual chat).

For you to ask Mom

What were your family's rules when you were growing up?

Did you agree with them? Why or why not?

What was one thing you didn't like about school?

Tell me about a time when you got in trouble at home or school.

If you could do one thing over again, what would it be and how would you do it differently?

For Mom to ask you

Which of our family's rules are the easiest for you to keep?

Which are the hardest?

If you were the mom of this family, what would you do differently than I do?

What's your very favorite thing to do?

What would you really like to do that you can't (because of your age or other reasons)?

 Checkpoint

What did you learn in this chapter about Mom or your relationship with her?

_____

_____

What did you learn about your relationship with God?

_____

_____

Do you know why Mom has her rules? How can you be sure, or how can you find out?

_____

_____

How can you be sure that God's rules are right? (Read Psalm 18:30)

_____

_____

Write a prayer about God's rules. Then tuck your prayer into the eighth envelope of your prayer chain.

Psst! You might think Mom enjoys yelling at you. In fact, Mom feels terrible about yelling, but most of the time she does it as a last resort. She probably asks God to show her a better way to handle her frustration. You can reduce the yelling by asking Mom to make sure you're paying attention when she tells you the first time, doing what she says the first time, and reminding her—in a calm, respectful voice—that she doesn't need to yell so much.

Bear with each other and forgive whatever grievances you may have against one another. Forgive as the Lord forgave you.

~ Colossians 3:13

FACT 9

Mom Forgives Me and I Forgive Mom.

Mom Forgives Me and I Forgive Mom.

I know because...

✴ Even if I'm really annoyed with her, I always get over it.

✴ She still hugs me, even if I'm acting grumpy.

✴ She puts "I'm sorry" notes in my backpack.

✴ God wants us to forgive each other.

You probably disagree with Mom over lots of things—large and small—several times a week. How do you resolve these disagreements? Do you...

✴ Say a few final, angry words and then walk away from each other?

✴ Stomp, slam doors and throw things?

✴ Stay mad and not talk at all for several hours until finally someone has to say something off the subject?

✴ Say "I'm sorry," forgive each other, and talk about the problem until it's resolved?

One of the most important things you can do as a Christian is forgive other people. Forgiving people when they treat you well is easy—what's hard is forgiving them when they hurt, disappoint or anger you.

If the following story sounds familiar, it's because you've read the Bible parable on which it is based (Matthew 18:22-35). Here it's been updated, but the meaning is the same. See what Ashley's mom is trying to teach her.

The Humongous Debt (a Parable)

Ashley had a catastrophe. She wanted to go to Kyla's birthday party, a sleepover. Kyla was one of the most popular girls at school, and this was the first time she'd invited Ashley to anything. It would be Ashley's second sleepover. (Her first had been at Shannon's, her best friend, just before Shannon moved to Australia.)

Ashley was all set to go to the sleepover…until the phone bill came. Because Ashley had been missing Shannon in Australia, she had called Shannon every night for a week. But when Mom and Dad saw the phone bill, they went crazy. Now she was grounded and she couldn't go to the sleepover. And that was the catastrophe.

No way in the world could Ashley pay for those phone calls. She'd have to save her allowance for the rest of her life, or baby-sit for 20 years, to pay that bill.

She was on a month-long "time out" (Mom's words) from just about everything—no allowance, no after-school activities, no TV or computer, no phone (of course). And no parties, including sleepovers.

The week before the party, Ashley tried one more time: "Please let me go, Mom. I'm so sorry I made all those calls. I won't ever do it again."

Her mother gave her the no-way look. "Ashley, what you did was inconsiderate and irresponsible. You showed no understanding of the value of money. It's not the way Dad and I are raising you."

Ashley didn't want to hear the lecture all over again—she felt bad enough already. Whenever she thought about the phone bill, her stomach felt woozy. She couldn't comprehend all that money. It was like trying to understand how God could be everywhere at the same time.

"I know, and I'm really sorry," Ashley said. "I didn't know it would cost so much."

And she meant it.

Mom paused, and Ashley felt a loophole growing in the punishment.

"Listen," Mom said. "I'm not taking away your punishment, just adjusting it since we already said you could go to the sleepover before all this happened. But you'll have to make up for it with an extra weekend of time out. No exceptions."

Ashley leaped around the kitchen, then twirled and hugged Mom. "Thank you, thank you, thank you!"

Ashley skipped off to her room, flopped on her bed and wrote a list for the sleepover:

Sleeping bag
PJs
CDs, DVDs
Birthday present for Kyla

Birthday present! How would she pay for a birthday present with no money? Her allowance had been cut off. Then she remembered that Brittany owed her money.

Ashley saw Brittany at school the next day. "I need that money you borrowed," she said sternly.

"I don't have it," Brittany said.

"What do you mean?" asked Ashley. "You've had it for weeks. Now I need it back."

"I'll pay you when I get it," said Brittany, frowning. "You never said when I had to pay you back."

"Sell something," Ashley suggested. "Sell that CD you bought. I heard Kerry say he liked it. Maybe he'll buy it from you."

"No way will I sell that. It's my favorite."

"If you don't give me back my money," Ashley said, "I'll tell your mother." She felt woozy again, knowing this wasn't how she should treat a friend. But she was desperate.

"You're nuts," Brittany said and walked away.

A few days later, Mom called Ashley into her bedroom. "Close the door, please," Mom said. "Come and sit next to me."

"I'm getting ready for the party," Ashley said.

"That's what I want to talk about. Brittany's mother told me you loaned Brittany some money. Is that true?"

Ashley nodded. "She needed it for a new CD." Here came that woozy feeling again.

Mum's The Word!

In Portuguese: Mamãe
In Russian: Mama
In Spanish: Mamá

"It's okay to lend money to your friends," Mom said gently. "What disturbs me is your trying to force Brittany to pay you back."

Ashley looked down at her hands. "I needed the money for Kyla's birthday present."

Mom sighed. "That was a horrible way to treat your friend."

"But she owed me, and I needed the money," said Ashley, her voice rising.

"If Brittany can't pay you back right now, you shouldn't have pressed her," said Mom.

"But where would I get the money?"

"You could have gone without a present."

"No way," said Ashley as tears started to fill her eyes. She'd never get invited to another party by the popular group if she showed up empty-handed.

"Well, it's not worth discussing because you're not going to the party now anyway," said Mom as she turned to leave Ashley's room.

"What? Mom!" Ashley cried.

"This sleepover meant so much to you, and you begged me to let you go, so I decided to let you off the hook," said Mom. "But it's obvious you didn't learn anything from my generosity. If you can't forgive your friend's measly debt, I won't forgive your humongous one."

Why was Ashley's mom so upset with Ashley?

_____

Do you agree with her mom's final decision? Why or why not?

_____

_____

Q: My mom gave away some books, old toys and clothes that I loved without asking me. I was so mad, I said I'd never forgive her. She said she's sorry, but I can't forget what she did. I still can't forgive her.

A: Your mom probably just forgot how you might feel about her cleaning out the clutter. She didn't do it purposely to hurt you or make you mad. The thing to remember is that no matter how much you can't or won't forgive her, God—who's greater than anything (including pain and anger)—has already forgiven her. Can't you, also forgive her? If you do, don't be surprised if you're still angry. Sometimes you have to forgive people many times before you've truly forgiven them. Jesus tells us to forgive a person "seventy-seven times" (Matthew 18:22). Give it time, and ask God for help, and you will feel the grudge go away.

Q: A long time ago, my mother did something pretty bad to me. Even though it's all over now and she has gotten help and hasn't done it again, I still feel deep inside that she will do it again someday. How can I get over this feeling?

A: It sounds like your mother has made a sincere effort to stop doing whatever she did that hurt you. But once something bad happens, it's hard to forget about it and not expect the same thing to happen again unexpectedly. Not knowing if or when it might happen can cause a lot of stress—even more than if you know for sure that it will happen. First, have you forgiven her for what she did a long time ago? Remember that forgiving someone doesn't mean you give permission to do it again. It means that you let go of the emotional energy it takes to stay angry at the person who wronged you. It also means you let God take that pain and anger from you so that you're not a slave to it anymore. Second, have you talked about your fears with your mother? It's important that she knows about them so she can be extra careful about her behavior. If it's still difficult for you to relax and enjoy your life, ask your mother (or father) to let you talk to a Christian counselor who can help you use God's wonderful healing power to restore the relationship with your mother that both of you deserve.

Q: My mom asked me to watch my baby brother for a minute while she went to the kitchen for his bottle. He was standing in his crib, and when I turned away for a second he flipped himself out of his crib and fell on the floor. My mother heard the noise and ran back to his room. She said, "I thought you said you would watch him!" Then right away she said, "I'm so sorry I said that. It wasn't your fault at all. I shouldn't have put you in charge." He was fine, but I was so shocked and upset that I started to cry. And now every time I think about what could have happened, I cry. He could have been hurt really badly and it would have been all my fault. How can I get my mother to forgive me? Now I want to start babysitting and earn some extra money, but I'm scared that something like that will happen again.

A: Your mother regretted what she said the moment those words left her mouth. If you asked her now, she'd probably tell you she wishes she hadn't made you feel you caused your brother to hurt himself. She said that because she was terrified for your brother and the words just flew out. Your mother forgave you a long time ago but she probably hasn't forgiven herself for leaving a young girl in charge of an energetic baby and making you feel that you were to blame. Ask God to take away your guilt and restore your confidence in your ability to take care of children. Because this happened, you'll be extra careful when you watch any babies. That's a plus! To help boost your confidence even more, read a few books about baby and child care, and take a babysitting class if one is available near you.

Mom and I write notes to each other when we're mad. It's easier to do that than yell or say nothing. I think more about what I'm going to say when I write.
—Brooke M.
age 9
Oregon

God Forgives Me (a gazillion times plus!)

It doesn't make sense to forgive someone who's done something hurtful or outright wrong to you. But think about this: God forgives you every day.

It could be for angry words you said to Mom.

It could be for a lie you told.

It could be for gossiping about a girl at church.

It could be for taking something that didn't belong to you.

It could be for ignoring someone who needed your help.

God could have stopped Jesus' death, but He didn't. He loves you. God wanted your sins to

My mom always says, "I'm sorry" over something she does. But I wish she'd just think about it first.
—Stacey S.
age 13
Florida

die with Jesus so you can spend eternity with Him.

When Jesus died, it was as if He wrote out a check for more money than is in the entire universe and handed it to God.

"This should cover it," Jesus said.

And God said, "Yup, their debts are all paid. They're all forgiven."

The greatest gift you'll ever receive is God's forgiveness. And, unlike Ashley's phone bill, it is a debt you can never pay back. Compared to the humongous debt that God has forgiven, any wrong that you should forgive would seem trivial.

Besides, it takes a lot of energy to carry around a grudge—you don't stop being hurt, angry and disappointed until you forgive. Giving that grudge to God takes away those bad feelings and makes you feel light and free!

It isn't always easy to forgive someone. Hurts do HURT deeply. But remember that God can do anything. If you don't have the desire, strength or courage to forgive someone, He will give you what you need. Ask Him to help, and He will.

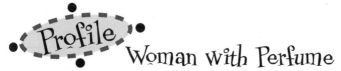

Woman with Perfume

Her name is: unknown

She lived in: possibly Bethany, a town near Jerusalem

One evening, when Jesus was having dinner at the home of a Pharisee (a Jewish religious leader), a woman in town dropped by. This woman was not a person with whom Mom would want you to hang out—she had the reputation for being "sinful."

The woman brought a jar of expensive perfume and stood behind Jesus, who was eating at the table, and cried. (Why do you think she was crying?) Her tears splashed on Jesus' feet, so she dried them with her long hair, and kissed them. Then she poured her expensive perfume on Jesus' feet.

The Pharisee—Jesus' host—thought Jesus must be a fake prophet. He figured if Jesus knew what kind of woman she was, He wouldn't let her do what she was doing to Him.

But Jesus knew exactly who she was! He said to His host, "When I came here tonight, you didn't give Me any water to wash My feet. You also didn't greet Me with a kiss. This woman, who you only see as sinful, washed and dried My feet and kissed them from the moment she entered. She even anointed Me with oil, which you did not. I'm telling you, because she loves Me so much and has faith in Me, all her sins are forgiven. She will not take this forgiveness for granted as some others do."

※ Read all about this woman in Luke 7:36-50.

Time Out! If there's something you've done that needs forgiveness, it will stand between you and God until you ask Him to forgive you. Ask God to show you what needs forgiveness. (Listen quietly, and He'll tell you.) Then, ask God to forgive you. Say, "Dear God, I'm sorry for (name the problem). Please forgive me and help me to not do it again." He will forgive you immediately!

1. Who in this story needed to ask for forgiveness?

_____

2. Although Jesus knew all about the woman with the perfume, why did He easily forgive her?

_____

3. Is there anything for which you need to ask Mom to forgive you? Right now, find her and say, "I'm sorry for (name the problem). Please forgive me." You can bet she will!

4. Is there anything for which you need to forgive Mom? Forgive her right now. (You don't have to tell Mom you've forgiven her, but it would make her feel great to hear you say it.)

When my sister and I fight, my mom makes one of us say, "I'm sorry" and the other say, "I forgive you." Sometimes we don't want to do it, but we still have to say it.

–Marissa H.
age 10
Delaware

 ## Read
✳ Matthew 18:21-35

Pray

Dear God, thank You for the gift of Jesus Christ and forgiving me long ago with His death on the cross. Please help me to forgive people, even when I don't want to or can't. Amen.

➤ Do It! ◄

Ping Pong Journal

A "Ping Pong Journal" is a fun name for a journal that you write with someone else. First you will write in it and give it to Mom. Then Mom will write in it and give it back to you. But before you start writing, you'll decorate the journal to make it uniquely yours.

There are many reasons for keeping a Ping Pong Journal, such as:

- Sometimes it's easier to write what you're thinking or feeling to someone.
- The other person isn't always around to talk when you want.
- It can be easier to read someone's feelings than to hear them.
- Writing gives you a wonderful keepsake of a conversation with another person.

 ## What You Need

* spiral-bound notebook
* fabric (large enough to cover front and back of notebook)
* white glue
* ribbon (2" longer than notebook)
* photo or drawing of you and Mom
* buttons, plastic gems, beads, ribbons, sequins, shells or other decorations
* pen or pencil

What to Do

1. Lay the fabric on a flat surface, right side down.

2. Place the notebook on the fabric. Line up the edge with the holes through which the spiral runs.

3. Using a pencil, trace around the three sides of the notebook on the fabric.

4. Repeat steps 2 and 3 on another piece of fabric. You now have two outlines of the notebook on the fabric: one for the front cover and one for the back.

5. Cut out both outlines.

6. Place the notebook on a flat surface with the front cover facing you.

7. Dot glue on the notebook cover, close to all the edges and then inside the edges.

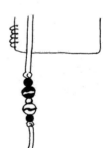

8. Place a fabric piece over the notebook cover. Pat and stretch it to cover the surface. Don't worry if it's too small in some places. If the fabric is too big, you can trim it after the glue dries.

9. Repeat steps 6 through 8 for the back cover.

10. Glue the photograph or drawing of you and Mom on the front cover.

11. Decorate the front of the journal with beads, buttons, ribbons or whatever else you want. (If the pages stick together with excess glue, gently separate them before the glue dries.)

12. Tie one end of the ribbon to the top spiral of the journal. Leave a 1-inch end at the top. (You can tie a colorful bead to this end.)

13. At the other end of the pre-cut ribbon, tie a knot about ½-inch past the bottom of the journal.

14. String some beads from the bottom of the ribbon. For the first bead (the one next to the knot), use one with a hole smaller than the knot, and end with a bead with a small hole. This will keep the beads from slipping over the knots.

15. Tie a final knot near the end of the ribbon.

Note: Let the journal dry completely before writing in it.

How to Keep a Ping Pong Journal with Mom

1. Decide how often you will each keep the journal before starting. Find a schedule that works for you both. For example, you might write on Monday and give it to Mom for her to return to you the next Monday.

2. Start slowly. Try four sentences for each entry. Then, move to six, and then a whole page.

3. Write honest thoughts and feelings. If Mom did something that embarrassed you, or if you want to ask her something you've been shy about asking in person, this is the place to do it. Hint: Write in pencil (you can erase if needed!).

4. When it's your turn to reply, think about your reply before writing it, especially if you read something that upsets you in any way.

5. Always pray before you start. You can say something like this: "Dear God, thank You for Mom (or my daughter), and thank You for giving us this special way to talk to each other. Help me find what I need to say to her, and please bless the words. Amen."

6. If you can't think of anything to write, here are some ideas to get you started:

- Copy a poem, or write your own.
- Write or copy a prayer.
- Copy a passage from Scripture that describes what you're feeling or thinking. Then explain why you chose that passage.
- Ask questions.
- Write a quiz.
- Draw or paste a cartoon or comic strip.
- Ask a riddle, or tell a joke.

The View

Time for an interview (or a casual chat).

For you to ask Mom

What two things are the hardest about being a Christian?

What did your mom tell you about forgiving other people?

When you were my age, did you ever have a fight with a friend? Were you able to make up? Why or why not?

Is there someone who hurt you and you haven't been able to forgive?

Is there something you've done for which you need forgiveness?

For Mom to ask you

What will your life be like when you're grown up?

What things can you do (and not do) to make that life come true?

For you, what's the hardest thing about forgiving people?

How do you feel when you do forgive someone?

If Jesus came to our house right now, is there anything for which you'd need to ask Him to forgive you?

✔ Checkpoint

What did you learn about Mom or your relationship with her?

_____

_____

What did you learn about your relationship with God?

_____

_____

Do you know Mom has forgiven you and will always forgive you?

_____

_____

How can you be sure, or how can you find out?

_____

_____

How does Mom know you forgive her?

_____

_____

How can you be sure God has forgiven you and will always forgive you? (Read Luke 6:37)

_____

_____

Write a prayer about this fact. Then, tuck your prayer into the ninth envelope of your prayer chain.

Psst! Mom prays every day for you. She prays that God will help her be a better mom. She asks Him what to say and not say to you, and what to teach you. She also asks God to forgive her for her mistakes as a mom. She even asks Him to protect you from her weaknesses and shortcomings.

"Love the Lord your God with all your heart and with all your soul and with all your mind and with all your strength." The second is this: "Love your neighbor as yourself."

~ Mark 12:30-31

FACT 10

Mom Needs My Help.

Mom Needs My Help

i know because...

❋ She hardly ever takes time out for fun.

❋ She has so much on her to-do list that she can't find her keys.

❋ I try to live the way she expects.

❋ I'm growing up and can handle more responsibilities.

If someone offered you a job in which you'd be a doctor, nutritionist, chef, chauffeur, referee, banker, teacher, prayer coach, maid, veterinarian, psychologist, tailor, personal shopper, hairstylist, coach and detective, and you had to do any or all of these things at one time all day, every day, would you accept the job?

Oh, and you would not be allowed to show that you were tired, frustrated, hurt, angry or sad. And you wouldn't get paid for it.

One last thing: you would love this job more than anything you'll ever do in your whole life. Now would you take the job?

This is what being a mom is all about. It's hard work, and Mom probably had no idea what she was getting into when she first started. She's gotten lots of on-the-job training and learned from her mistakes. Just when she feels confident about being a mom to kids at a certain age, they grow up a little and present a whole new set of things for her to learn. You can bet that this job makes her feel humble and she says lots of prayers every day and night for you and her.

My dad died last year. I miss him so much! My mom used to not let us sleep in her bed at all, but now she lets us sleep with her on Saturday nights. We watch videos together in bed. Sometimes we watch videos we made with my dad so we can remember him.

—Hannah V.
age 9
New Hampshire

But being a mom doesn't mean doing the job all by herself. Another part of her job is "project manager," which means she decides how you can help her. If she doesn't ask for your help, she could end up in bed from sheer exhaustion.

If you don't help Mom when she asks, you could miss out on some great rewards. You probably remember the story of the Little Red Hen. Check out a modern version of this classic tale below.

The Little Red Hen (and Her Daughters)

"Girls, would someone bring me the hammer?" called Mom from the patio. It was the first warm day of spring, and Mom was setting up the gazebo.

"Not me," said Tiffany from the couch. "Jennifer, you get it."

"Not me," said Jennifer from the computer. "Tiffany, you get it."

"Guess I'll get it myself," said Mom and went to the garage for the toolbox.

A little later, Mom asked, "Girls, will you come out and hold this up for me?"

"Not me," said Tiffany. "You do it, Jennifer."

"Not me," said Jennifer. "You do it, Tiffany."

"Guess I'll do it all by myself," said Mom as she struggled to get each heavy side of the gazebo to stand.

"There," she said and came in the house. "Who wants to help make lemonade?"

"Not me," said Tiffany. "You do it, Jennifer."

"Not me," said Jennifer. "You do it, Tiffany."

"Fine," said Mom, eyeing both of them. "I'll do it all by myself."

An hour later, Tiffany's movie was over, and Jennifer's eyes were tired from staring at the computer screen.

"Where's Mom?" Tiffany asked.

"I was gonna ask you the same thing," said Jennifer.

"Out here," said Mom.

The girls opened the back door and stepped out. Mom lay under the shade of the gazebo, stretched out on a patio chair, reading a book. A pitcher of icy lemonade sat on a table beside her and the portable radio played jazzy music.

The girls could already taste that cold, sweet lemonade. "I'll get another glass," Tiffany said.

"Get two," Jennifer said.

"Nope," said Mom.

"Huh?"

"I worked for it all by myself and I'm going to enjoy it all by myself. Besides, it's time you two started that weeding you promised."

The sisters looked at each other.

"Sorry, Mom," said Tiffany.

"Yeah, sorry," said Jennifer. "But, can you help us find the garden gloves?"

Does that story sound familiar from your life? If it does, it might be because when you were a helpless baby, Mom did everything for you. She changed your diapers; nursed, fed and bathed you; dressed you and washed your clothes; held, kissed and worried about you. She did all these things day and night, over and over.

As you got older, she continued to take care of you. She kept your fingers out of the outlets, made sure you didn't swallow quarters, stopped the dog from slobbering on your face, and kept you from falling out of your crib and then your "big-girl" bed. She drove you to day care, preschool or the babysitter. She still worried about you.

Then one day Mom said, "Hmmm, she can get her own spoon. She can pick up her own clothes. She can even put her own dishes in

Mum's The Word!

In Swahili: Mama
In Swedish: Moder
In Tibetan: Ka-ta
In Yiddish: Mamme

the dishwasher and sweep the floor."

But by then you'd gotten used to her doing things for you–and you liked it. Why spoil a sweet deal? you thought. So you kept asking, "Mom, would you (fill in the blank) for me?"

Mom knows that God wants her to take care of you, but she also knows He wants her to prepare you to take care of yourself. And that day is coming soon!

Q: I was very sick when I was in second grade. Now my mom protects me so much that I can't do anything for myself or help her do things. It makes me feel like a sick person again, which I'm not. How can I make her stop?

A: You must be an amazing daughter, because most girls don't complain when their moms won't let them help out. But no one likes to feel helpless and dependent on other people. Your mom is still worried that something might happen to you if you overexert yourself. If your doctor has told her you can do anything a girl your age can do, then show her you can handle it. Start by doing light chores without her asking you to do them. Then offer to help her in other ways, such as gardening, cooking or washing the car. When she sees you're okay, she'll give you more freedom, and she might stop worrying about you as much.

Q: My mother is a single mom. She works until dinnertime. Our house is always a mess, and I'm embarrassed to bring my friends over. I always make excuses when they ask if they can come over. Instead of cleaning the house, my mother hangs out on the couch or in her room. What can I do?

A: You're embarrassed because your mother doesn't keep the house clean enough for your friends? What are you doing to help her? You could clean up the house while she's still at work.

You could pick up, do dishes, vacuum, do laundry, even make a simple dinner. You can also help her by getting her off the couch. Suggest that you both go for a walk, take a bike ride or go in-line skating together. It will help her get the exercise she needs for doing her job, and it can help chase away some of the blues she might be feeling (taking care of a home, family and job all by herself is a huge responsibility!). It will also give you two more fun time together.

Q: I'm really busy. I go to school, band practice, two clubs, swimming and youth group meetings. My mother keeps telling me she needs my help, but when do I have the time to help?

A: Have you ever heard the expression "If you need something done, ask a busy person?" This means that someone who has a lot to do must be very organized and could fit one more task into her schedule. You say you don't have time, but you'd be amazed at how little time some tasks take. For example, you can empty the dishwasher in three minutes and load it with dirty dishes in another three. You can make your bed in one minute and feed the dog in 30 seconds. It takes a lot more time to stress or complain about doing these tasks than to actually do them. You'll find that you have several minutes here and there in your busy day to do such things. But if you don't, and your mom continues to need your help, you should think about easing up on your activities and clubs so that you can help her.

God Needs My Help

God works through you to give His love to others. When you love God and your neighbor, you obey the two commandments that Jesus called "the greatest" commandments (Mark 12:30-31).

You don't have to go on an overseas missions trip or even work at a homeless shelter every week to help God. You can start at home with Mom—there's plenty to do there!

You can help God by:

* Thinking about what you say to Mom before you say it.
* Doing your chores and homework before Mom has to remind you.
* Being really honest with Mom about your feelings.
* Holding Mom's hand, patting her back and hugging her.
* Reading to your younger brother or sister before bed, or helping at bath time.
* Taking responsibility for family pets (feeding, walking, bathing, grooming).
* Letting your sib get the last word in an argument (even if you can't stand it!).
* Acting in ways that show respect and honor for Mom (and Dad).

When you help Mom, you help God and you obey His two greatest commandments.

Girl Talk!

My friend had invited me to her church. I really liked it, but the rest of my family aren't Christians and I felt weird going to church without them. So I started praying that my mother would come just once. Then one day she asked, "What's it like at church?" So I told her what I liked about it. Then the next Sunday she came with me!

—Minna R.
age 13
Virginia

Mrs. Noah

Her name means: We don't know her name, but "Noah" in Hebrew means "comfort."

Lived in: probably around southeast Turkey

Husband: Noah

Sons: Shem, Ham and Japheth

God was furious that people did whatever they wanted, ignoring what He wanted. So He told Noah to build an ark (a kind of boat) and put two of every kind of animal in it. God was going to flood the earth and destroy every living thing, then start the earth all over again.

"Take your family, too," God said.

Mrs. Noah (Noah's wife) had seven days to prepare for the trip. Imagine what it would have been like to be on a boat with a husband, three sons and their wives, and two of every kind of animal! Not only did she need to stock food for the people on the boat, she needed to bring enough food to keep the animals happy for 40 days.

After everyone was in the boat for weeks, they probably started to get bored, and then bickered and argued with each other just to pass the time. It would have been like a really long road trip or camping trip, except there was no radio, TV, fast-food restaurants, movies, malls—nothing to keep them busy or entertained.

Mrs. Noah had a huge responsibility keeping everyone happy and out of each other's faces. Maybe she

My mom went back to work because my dad hasn't been able to find a job in a year. A lot of my friends' parents have lost their jobs. Mom says we should thank God for her job and all the blessings we have. I'd just like to ask God to give everyone a job.

—Rose H.
age 11
Connecticut

organized family evenings and chore charts. Maybe everyone got together (after all the animals were fed and their pens were cleaned) and told stories or jokes, or played charades or "Go Fish." Maybe they sang songs like "Row, Row, Row Your Boat" (in a round, of course!).

When God told Noah to take his family on the ark with him, God made a promise to Noah's family that he would take care of them and give them whatever they needed. In doing this, God showed moms and dads even today how important it is to take care of their children, especially when everything around them is uncertain.

When the flood was over and the ark was set on the Ararat mountains, everyone got out and walked on land for the first time since the rain began. Mrs. Noah became the only mother left on earth. Every person born after that flood came from her family.

✳ Read more about Mrs. Noah in: Genesis 6 to 8.

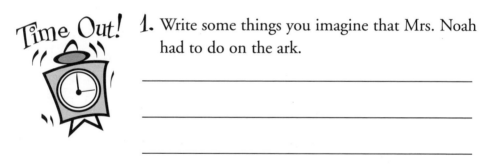

Time Out! 1. Write some things you imagine that Mrs. Noah had to do on the ark.

_____

_____

_____

2. On the next page, make a list of five things you can do this week to help Mom. If you can't think of anything, here are some ideas:

- Set the dinner table.
- Give in to your brother or sister before one of you has to call out, "Mom!"
- Study that hard subject an extra 20 minutes each night to improve your grade.
- Agree willingly when she says no (instead of nagging, whining or begging).

_____

_____

_____

3. List five things you can do this week to help God. Some ideas:

- Take your neighbors' trash can to their gate after pickup.
- Listen to your music quietly (or with headphones).
- Greet your family and the first three people you see in the morning with a cheery "Good morning!"
- Think of five people for whom you can pray, and pray for them.
- Look at the list for #1 above!

_____

_____

_____

4. At the end of the week, look at your lists, and check off the items you did. Add new items to replace them. Try doing this for three weeks, until helping becomes a habit.

Read
✳ James 2:14-19

Pray

Dear God, thank You for my mom and dad, who gave me life. Thank You for everyone who helps me with their words, actions and prayers. Show me where I can help in return. Amen.

~➤ Do It! ←~

Coupon Crackers

You've probably heard the saying "good things come in small packages." Often, the gifts people remember most don't cost much at all, but they do show a lot of love. One way you and Mom can give each other small but thoughtful and loving presents is with coupons. Deliver your coupons in a fun, festive way by putting them into Coupon Crackers (like the Christmas crackers from British tradition). Learn all about making coupons and crackers on the following pages.

☞ What You Need

* ✳ coupons on pages 171 and 173
* ✳ scissors
* ✳ pen
* ✳ toilet tissue tube (or any tube cut to 4½ inches)
* ✳ tissue paper, any color (12 inches square or larger)
* ✳ ruler
* ✳ pencil
* ✳ stickers
* ✳ gift ribbon
* ✳ hard candy, coins or other trinkets (optional)

◎ What to Do

1. Cut out the coupons.
2. Fill them out with what you want to give Mom (see lots of ideas on the next page). For example, you could give her a coupon for

her choice of music in the car. When Mom's in the mood for her music, she will return the coupon to you. (You can also make your own coupons by hand or on a computer. Make them as fancy as you want, using different fonts and colors, stickers, doodles or clip art. The most important point about coupons is they're written in love!

3. Be sure to do what the coupon says!

Coupon Ideas to Try

- ❀ A video-and-popcorn night together
- ❀ Chores you aren't normally expected to do
- ❀ Talking about what's on your mind
- ❀ One medium pizza
- ❀ Breakfast in bed
- ❀ A manicure (in a salon or at home)
- ❀ Dancing to old-fashioned music
- ❀ A hug
- ❀ A picnic on the living-room floor
- ❀ Going bike riding or in-line skating, or taking a walk together
- ❀ Listening (and not talking) for 10 minutes
- ❀ One "I'm sorry"
- ❀ Watching Saturday-morning TV together snuggled in bed
- ❀ 15 minutes of just being silly
- ❀ Lunch out
- ❀ A completely honest answer to your question
- ❀ A story
- ❀ A song
- ❀ A joke
- ❀ A prayer

4. To make the cracker, measure the tube halfway (2¼ inches), and cut it in half to make two shorter tubes.

5. Lay the tissue paper on a flat surface and use a ruler to measure 12 inches by 12 inches. Mark the dimensions with a pencil. Cut out the tissue paper square.

6. Place strips of double-sided tape along the length of the two tubes, about 1 inch apart.

7. Fold the paper square in half, and crease it lightly, so you can see where the center of the paper is. Then place the paper in front of you on a flat surface, with the crease running vertically (up and down).

8. Place the tubes together (as if they were still one tube) at the edge of the paper closest to you, with the space between the tubes at the paper's center crease.

9. Carefully roll the tubes along the paper. When all the paper is rolled around the tubes, fasten the edge of the paper with a few pieces of double-sided tape.

10. Twist the paper closed around one end of the tube. (Follow the same direction as you rolled to keep the paper smooth.)

11. Use ribbon to tie a bow around the twisted end.

12. Fold up the filled-in coupon, and place it in the tube from the other end. Add any other items you want into the tube.

13. Twist the other end of the paper closed, and tie a bow around it.

14. Using a toothpick, pierce a row of holes through the paper at the center (where the tubes are separated). This will make the cracker easier to open. Pierce carefully so that you don't tear the paper open.

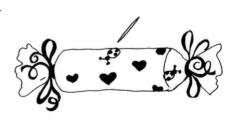

15. Decorate the cracker with stickers, markers, sequins or whatever you'd like.

16. To open the cracker, hold each side and twist gently as you pull the tubes apart.

The View

Time for an interview (or a casual chat).

For you to ask Mom

What three things can I do to help you more?

When you were my age, what were your chores?

How do you help God?

When you were growing up, for what did you need help that you didn't get?

What did you and your mom do for fun together?

For Mom to ask you

Which chore do you like the most? Why?

Which one do you like the least? Why?

What device would you like to invent to make something easier to do?

What three things can I do to help you?

What fun things do we do together? What would you like to do with me for fun?

✓ Checkpoint

What did you learn about Mom or your relationship with her?

_____

_____

What did you learn about your relationship with God?

_____

_____

Do you know Mom needs your help? How can you be sure, or how can you find out? _____

_____

How can you help God? (Read Matthew 28:18-20) _____

_____

Write a prayer about this fact. Then tuck your prayer into the tenth envelope of your prayer chain.

Psst! After you go to bed, Mom stays up another two to three hours to finish off her day and prepare for the next day. She's so tired! But, once everyone is in bed, she has an hour or so to wind down after the long day. She may read in bed or soak in the tub or watch some TV. She's tired, but it's the only time of the day she has completely to herself.

This is the confidence we have in approaching God: that if we ask anything according to his will, he hears us. And if we know that he hears us—whatever we ask—we know that we have what we asked of him.

~ 1 John 5:14-15

Mom Is Always on My Side

Mom Is Always on My Side

i know because...

❋ She cheers at all my games, even when we're losing.

❋ She tells me she'll always love me.

❋ She takes the time to explain things I don't understand.

❋ She's prayed for me since before I was born.

Bear mothers do it, lion mothers do it, even blue jay mothers fight for their young. So it shouldn't shock you to know that Mom would do anything to protect and defend you, her child.

It may not seem at times like she's on your side–especially if all she seems to do is nag, criticize and discipline from morning to night–but she'll be as fierce as any bear, lion or even blue jay mother when it comes to protecting you.

A Mystery

"Mom!" Jenna called, slamming the front door. Today was Mom's fellowship meeting, but Jenna hoped she was still home.

Jenna's mom noticed Jenna's wet cheeks and red, puffy eyes.

"What's wrong?" Mom asked.

"The kids on the trip committee think I stole the car wash money," cried Jenna. "Even Mr. Watson treated me a little weird."

"You'd never steal money."

"I was supposed to take it to the bank. I should have right away, but I didn't. And I don't know where it is."

Mom went to the phone. "I just need to call Mrs. Kim to tell her I'll miss our group today."

Jenna stopped crying for a moment. "Mom, you love that group."

Mom sighed. "But you're more important."

As her mom made the call, Jenna felt relief wash over her, calming her anxiety. Whatever happened, she knew Mom would be with her.

Mom finished the call. "Now, think about what happened. Let's go through everything, step by step. How did you get the money?"

"Jacob gave it to me after geography. It was in a manila envelope."

Jenna thought about what happened next. "I took the envelope…"

Fresh tears streamed down Jenna's cheeks. "I don't remember, and it was more than $200. Maybe I dropped it!"

Mom set some crackers and juice on the table. Mom always knew what to do. Just being with her and knowing she believed in Jenna made Jenna feel so much better.

There was a boy in my Sunday school class who kept bothering me. I didn't want to go to church anymore because of him. Mom kept asking me about it so I finally told her why. I think she must have told my Sunday school teacher because the boy stopped bothering me after that.

*—Marta H.
age 13
North Carolina*

"Where did you go after Jacob gave you the envelope?" Mom asked.

"We ran to my locker because it was lunch and I was starving. So I unlocked my locker and…put it under my math notebook. Mom! I think it's still in my locker!"

"Great!" Mom smiled. "You can take it to the bank tomorrow."

Jenna gave her mom a big hug and went to call Jacob. "Oh, and you can still make your meeting!" exclaimed Jenna.

Q: I'm 13, and there's a guy I like who's 15. He asked me out, but my mom said no way until I'm at least 16. Some of my friends go out on dates. How can I get her to let me go?

A: It may not seem like it to you, but your mom is on your side. She knows you're too young to date, even if your friends are doing it now. She probably thinks it's fine to have boys as friends, but she's right not to let you have boyfriends now. Acting more grown up seems like fun, and it will be when you're older. But for now, keep in mind that your mom does know what's best for you. Consider a compromise: ask your mom if your guy can come over for pizza and movies.

Q: It doesn't feel like my mom is on my side at all. She's always on Dad's side. She agrees with every decision he makes about what I want. I feel like I can't do anything.

A: Your mom and dad are doing exactly the right thing by agreeing on how to answer your requests. They know that if they disagree in front of you, you'll ask one and then the other until you get the answer you want. Instead of playing one parent against the other (which is not honest and not the way God wants you to treat your parents), try asking them together at the same time. If you feel the answer they give you is unfair, explain the situation in more detail and explain your point of view. That's the more direct, mature and loving way to do things. If they still don't give you the answer you want, accept it and know that whether or not they say yes, they are both still on your side. The answer they give you is one they believe is right for you. Be grateful that your parents agree on how to raise you, because it's a sign that they love and respect each other.

Q: My stepmother is absolutely not on my side. She's so nice to her own kids but I often feel left out. I don't expect her to love me as much as my mom does, but she could at least act like she likes me.

A: That's a difficult situation to be in because each of you in the family is trying to adjust to this situation the best way you know how. You have three parents and new step-siblings to deal with. There could be several reasons for why your stepmother seems to be favoring her own kids, none of which mean she doesn't like you. One, she might be timid about disciplining you, thinking that it's your dad's and mom's jobs to do that. She doesn't want to step on their toes. Two, she may just not know you well enough to know how to treat you. Three, maybe she's cautious about looking like she's trying to win you over or take your mom's place. Is your stepmother generally nice to other people? If so, then she probably wants to have a close relationship with you, too. It sounds like it's time for you two to have a heart-to-heart talk. Tell her how you feel without accusing her

Girl Talk!

After an audition for my first play, I didn't get a callback for a dancer part, and I cried for hours. My mom told me how she didn't get into color guard, and the second time she tried, she got in. She said you have to keep trying and never give up.

—Haley C.
age 10
North Carolina

of things you don't know are true. Then listen to what she says.

Make some guidelines about your relationship. For example, if she wants to hug you, will you let her, and vice versa? Is she allowed to discipline you, and to what extent? When should your dad get involved? Pay attention to your own behavior, too. Make sure you're not disrespecting her authority as a parent by ignoring her and obeying only your dad or mom. Make sure that you're not hogging your dad's attention and time. Give him and your stepmother time together as a couple, and give your dad time with your step-sibs. Make the best effort you can to get along with her. Your relationship with her and your new sisters and brothers will last your whole life. The more successful you are now, the longer and stronger those bonds will be as you all grow older. And as with everything, pray to God and ask for His guidance in this situation.

God Is Always on (and by) My Side

When God led the Hebrew people out of slavery in Egypt, He brought them to the desert (Exodus 16).

If you've ever been to a desert, you know it's very dry. Water is scarce, which means edible plants are hard to find. An irrigation system is necessary to grow crops. The days are scorching hot and the temperature at night can drop to below freezing. Poisonous snakes and insects live in some deserts. It's not easy to live in the desert!

But God's people lived there for 40 years. God gave them everything they needed: tents to live in, clothes to wear, water to drink and food–called "manna," which he showered on them once a day like snow–to sustain them.

As the Hebrew people traveled through the desert, staying a few nights here and a few nights there, God showed them where to go. During the day, He became a pillar of cloud, and at night He was a pillar of fire, giving them warmth and light. Whether He was a cloud by day or fire by night, He never left them. God never abandoned His people!

Just as God took care of the Hebrews' every need thousands of years ago, He does the same for you today. He takes you out of slavery to what's wrong and shows you where the wonderful, safe places are.

God is always on your side, no matter what you do or where you are. And, He's always at your side. You know because He says, "Never will I leave you; never will I forsake you." (Hebrews 13:5)

Profile: The Shunammite Mom

Lived in: Shunem, north of Jezreel

Mom of: A son she adored

Wife of: A wealthy man

A rich woman who lived in Shunem wanted more than anything to have a child. This was the deepest prayer in her heart.

She and her husband began to invite the prophet Elisha to stay at their house whenever he was in Shunem. Elisha, who had performed many miracles through the power of God, knew the Shunammite woman wanted a baby. On one visit, he told her she would have a baby by the same time the following year.

Because the woman's desire for a baby was so great, she didn't want to believe what he said was true. She knew if he was lying, she'd be heartbroken when no baby appeared.

But just as Elisha had said, within a year the woman and her husband had a baby boy.

One morning when the boy was a few years old, he ran out to his father in the fields and cried, "My head. It hurts!"

The father, knowing that his wife's loving touch always comforted their son, told a servant to take the boy to his mother. She held him in her lap and tried to make him feel better, but he died.

Imagine how grief stricken she felt, losing the son she'd wanted all her life. She would have done anything to get him back.

So the woman decided to go to the person who knew about the boy long before he was ever born. First, she carried her dead son upstairs to the guest room and laid him on the bed in the room where Elisha stayed whenever he was in town.

Then she left to go find Elisha. She knew he was the only person who could help her. Crazy as it might sound, she wasn't going to give up without trying every possibility.

My mom and I have a special kiss that we do at bedtime, when we pray and when we say good-bye. We kiss and then touch our cheeks two times, then we touch our noses and our chins and foreheads, and then we kiss again and hug.

—June R.
age 9
Texas

She found Elisha on Mount Carmel and told him the story. Elisha told his servant to take Elisha's staff (a walking and herding stick) back to the woman's house and place it on her son's head. (The staff would take the place of Elisha.)

Elisha told the boy's mom to go with his servant.

"No," she said. "I'll only go with you."

So Elisha's servant set out for the woman's house, followed by Elisha and the boy's mother.

When the servant laid the staff on the boy's head, it did no good. The boy was still dead. When Elisha and the woman arrived, Elisha went up to the bedroom and closed the door. He prayed while lying on the boy. Soon, the boy's body grew warm, he sneezed seven times and came back to life.

When his mom saw her precious son alive again, she bowed down in thanks to Elisha and to God.

✳ Read more about the Shunammite mother in
  2 Kings 4:8-37 and 2 Kings 8:1-6.

Time Out!

1. How did the Shunammite mother show that she was on her son's side?

_____

_____

_____

2. Write about a time when Mom showed you she was on your side.

_____

_____

_____

3. Write about a time when you showed Mom you were on her side.

_____

_____

_____

4. Write about a time when God showed you He was on your side.

_____

_____

_____

Read

✳ Exodus 14:13-31

Pray

Dear God, thank You for never changing, even though everything else does. Thank You for Mom, who believes in me in the good times and sticks with me through the bad. Help me to show her I'm always on her side, too. Amen.

➤ Do It! ◄

Fragrant Sachet

In 2 Corinthians, the apostle Paul wrote about the knowledge of Christ as a "fragrance" which God spreads to others through us. We often recall people, places and events when we remember a scent from that time. Make this Fragrant Sachet for Mom to remind her of you.

☞ What You Need

✳ 3" x 6" piece of stiff, sheer fabric

✳ 3" length of narrow ribbon

✳ potpourri

✳ straight pins

✳ needle and thread

 **What to Do**

Trace and Cut Out the Sachet Shape

1. Trace the rectangle onto a piece of paper, and cut out the shape.

2. Pin the paper to the fabric.

3. Cut out the rectangle from the fabric, and remove the pins.

Sew the Sachet

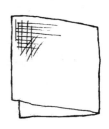

1. Fold the fabric in half, to make a square (fold so the wrong side of the fabric is outside and the right side is inside). If your fabric doesn't seem to have a "right" or "wrong" side, don't worry which side is facing you.

2. Pin the edges together along two adjoining sides. Don't pin the folded side. Leave one side (which will be the top) open.

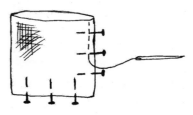

3. Thread the needle, tie a knot at the end, and use a running stitch (in and out in small stitches) to sew the two pinned edges. Keep your stitches about a ¼-inch from the edge of the fabric.

4. Take out the pins and turn the sachet right-side out.

Fill the Sachet

1. Put some potpourri (get it at a craft store or most department stores) loosely into the sachet until it is filled. If the pieces are very large, you can crush them into smaller ones.

2. Close the top of the sachet by carefully folding the top edges inside, pinning the folds down and then pinning the two folded edges together.

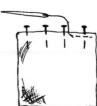

3. Sew the folded edges together. Take out the pins.

Finishing Touches

1. Tie a small bow with the ribbon. Trim the ends.

2. Sew or glue the bow onto the sachet.

3. Keep your sachet in a drawer, closet, or linen cupboard to make everything smell fragrant.

The View

Time for an interview (or a casual chat).

For you to ask Mom

Tell me about a time when your mom stuck up for you.

Was there a time when she didn't stick up for you and you wish she had?

Who is your hero, and why?

Tell me about a time when you really knew God was watching out for you.

When you feel misunderstood, what do you do?

For Mom to ask you

Was there a time when you knew I stuck up for you?

Was there a time when you knew I didn't stick up for you but should have?

Was there a time when I embarrassed you by being on your side?

Tell me about a time when you really felt God was watching out for you.

What do you do when you feel misunderstood?

> **Mum's The Word!**
>
> In Navajo: Mah
> In Norwegian: Mor
> In Persian: Mâmâ
> In Polish: Matka

 Checkpoint

What did you learn about Mom or your relationship with her?

_____

_____

What did you learn about your relationship with God?

_____

_____

How can you be sure Mom is on your side, or how can you find out?

_____

_____

How does Mom know you're on her side? _____

_____

How can you be sure God is on your side? (Read Exodus 13:22.)

_____

_____

Write a prayer about this fact. Then, tuck your prayer into the last envelope of your prayer chain.

Psst! Did you notice that many of the words for "mom" in different languages begin with or contain the "m" sound? That's because "m" is one of the first sounds babies make when they're learning to talk. If you listen to a young baby, you hear her or him say "ma-ma-ma" or "um-um-um" a lot. Knowing that, who do you think might have created the word for "mom" in all the different languages? Chances are, the babies did!

Bar*mom*eter 2

Now that you're almost finished with this book, take some time to think about what you've read, done and learned. Remember the survey you took at the beginning of this book? You'll take a similar one here. But this time, answer the questions based on what you've learned about Mom since you began working with the book. (And ask Mom to answer the same questions about you.)

1. Look at the "Bar*mom*eter 1" survey you took at the beginning of this book. Which questions would you answer differently now and how would you answer them?

_____

_____

_____

2. On the next page, draw a picture below of Mom the way you see her (or think of her) now. If you don't want to draw, you can glue a picture from a magazine or use a photograph.

AFTER Picture of Mom

3. Is this picture any different from the "before" picture? What made the difference?

_____

_____

_____

Finished with your prayer chain? Keep it hanging up to remind you of the Mom Facts. Or, put it in a drawer or some other place. In a few months, look at each prayer you wrote, and think about how God has answered it.

This coupon is given to: _____

For: _____

Because: _____

Expires on: _____

Signed: _____

Date: _____

This coupon is given to: _____

For: _____

Because: _____

Expires on: _____

Signed: _____

Date: _____

This coupon is given to: _____

For: _____

Because: _____

Expires on: _____

Signed: _____

Date: _____

This coupon is given to: _____

For: _____

Because: _____

Expires on: _____

Signed: _____

Date: _____

This coupon is given to: _____

For: _____

Because: _____

Expires on: _____

Signed: _____

Date: _____

This coupon is given to: _____

For: _____

Because: _____

Expires on: _____

Signed: _____

Date: _____

This coupon is given to: _____

For: _____

Because: _____

Expires on: _____

Signed: _____

Date: _____

This coupon is given to: _____

For: _____

Because: _____

Expires on: _____

Signed: _____

Date: _____

L48220

THE GIRL'S GUIDE TO LIFE

Ages 10–12, 192 pages, Paperback, Illustrated, Plus Bonus Free Add-On Gift. *The Girl's Guide to Life* is for girls who want a road map to lead them through life's journey. *The Girl's Guide to Life* points to the Bible, the best map of all, talks about issues girls face like family, friends, boys, school, money, nutrition, fitness, and standing firm when temptations appear. Ages 10–12.

THE CHRISTIAN GIRL'S GUIDE FOR PRETEENS

Ages 10–12, 176-208 pages, Paperback, Illustrated, Plus Bonus Free Add-On Gift. Encourage girls with these fun and creative books covering issues that matter most to preteens: fashion, being their best, making friends, understanding the Bible, getting along with Mom, dealing with money, and LIFE! Ages 10–12.

L48213

L48211

L48212

L48213

L48214

L48215

L48216

L48217

L48218

L48219

GOD'S GIRLS Fun Crafts Plus Devotions!

Ages 9–12, 184 pages, Paperback, Illustrated. Preteen girls will be captivated by this book, with devotions about Biblical women and crafts created especially for girls. Weaving belts, decorating rooms and party planning activities all teach girls that fun and faith are part of God's plan. Ages 9–12.

L48011

THE GOD AND ME!® BIBLE

Ages 6–9, 192 pages, Paperback, Full Color Illustrations. Designed to capture the vivid imaginations of growing girls, The God and Me! Bible puts God's Word inot the hearts and minds. The bright illustrations, creative activities, puzzles, and games that accompany each Bible story make learning important Bible truths both fun and easy. Ages 6–9.

L48522

JUST FOR ME! FOR GIRLS

Ages 6–9, 152 pages, Paperback, Illustrated, Plus Bonus Free Add-On Gift Through Stories, crafts, and fun activities, younger girls will discover what they need to grow closer to God! Ages 6–9.

L48413

L48412

L48411

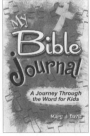

GUIDED JOURNALS FOR GIRLS AND BOYS

Ages 10–12, 136–160 pages, Paperback, Illustrated. Preteen boys and girls will love these daily devotional journals that really encourage them to dig into the Bible.

L46911   **DB46731**

Find more great stuff by visiting our website: **www.Rose-Publishing.com**